Rev. Rose Jacques

Unlocking REVELATION

THE SIMPLE TRUTH ABOUT THE BOOK OF REVELATION

Second Edition Revision

REV. ROSE JACQUES

TATE PUBLISHING
AND ENTERPRISES, LLC

Published by Tate Publishing & Enterprises, LLC
127 E. Trade Center Terrace | Mustang, Oklahoma 73064 USA
1.888.361.9473 | www.tatepublishing.com

Tate Publishing is committed to excellence in the publishing industry. The company reflects the philosophy established by the founders, based on Psalm 68:11,
"The Lord gave the word and great was the company of those who published it."

Cover design by Joana Quilantang
Interior design by Jomar Ouano
Cover Illustration by: Emily Brunner – used with permission
Interior Images: © 2015 Rev. Rose Jacques – used with permission

Published in the United States of America

ISBN: 978-1-68164-709-8
1. Religion / Biblical Studies / New Testament
2. Religion / Biblical Studies / Prophecy
15.06.24

DEDICATIONS AND ACKNOWLEDGMENTS

Dedicated to my Lord Jesus Christ, or Yehoshua, for whome this book was published. I am intrusting the later harvest to him.

To all my children, Thomas, Shawn, Shannine, and Edward. My grandchildren, Tyler, Caitlyn, Alyssa, Alexis and Dylan. Also to my spiritual children, and seed, both in Heaven and on Earth.

Warm thanks to all who proofed my book for me, my brother Doug Jacques, and all those who are now translating it in other languages.

A special thanks to my friend Emily Brunner for painting a beautiful cover picture.

Especially to the Alpha, and Omega, the Holy Spirit, and angels which woke me up and guided me through this whole process. My warmest love, and God's blessings on you all.

INSIGHT INTRODUCTION

TIME IS VERY SHORT

This is an insight into the coming of our Lord, Jesus Christ (whose real name is Yehoshua), but so many only know Him as Jesus, so I will use this name.

> *"And I went unto the angel, and said unto him, Give me the little book. And he said unto me, Take it, and eat it up; and it shall make thy belly bitter, but it shall be in thy mouth sweet as honey."* **(Rev. 10:9)**

This book will hopefully wake up not only the body of believers, but those on the fence, to get ready. It is based on a real dream and visions given to me, by the Holy Spirit, shortly after the first sighting, of the four blood moon warning, in 2014. Without the Spirit of the Living God, there is no way these prophesy's unfolding today, could have been known by Apostle John, a Believer in Jesus as the true Messiah, almost two thousand years ago. The book of Revelation was meant to be open only now, when time is very close.

This book covers God's true Appointed Worship Day, how to change our DNA, preparing for Christ's coming, and the true meaning of the book of Revelation.

I have a lot more insight I could share with you, but I do not want to burden you in one book. We have but a short time now, to get what is important out to all. Look around and you will see many, Jesus Bride, prophesying of His soon coming. My voice is here, unlocking the book of Revelation. Gods message to me, for all.

> *"And it shall come to pass in the last days, saith God, I will pour out of my Spirit upon all flesh: and your sons and your daughters shall prophesy, and your young men shall see visions, and your old men shall dream dreams: And on my servants and on my handmaidens I will pour out in those days of my Spirit; and they shall prophesy:"* **(Acts 2:17)**

Please stand with me, and help get the word out, and prepare for the greatest event ever to come.

Order book at: unlockingrevelation.tateauthor.com

God keep you,

Rose Jacques

TABLE OF CONTENTS

1. MY DREAMS AND VISIONS

Revelation was written in 95 AD, so all these prophesies are for us now, and clearly was not written for those in the destruction of Jerusalem in 70 AD. There is a growing teaching that is trying to lull young Christians into believing the whole Bible is all about what happened in the destruction of Jerusalem in 70 AD. Implying to forget the end, and anything scary, just build your life. Really? I wish it were that easy. This future destruction will be global, and much greater. Remember, Satan's kingdom must be locked up forever, but is clearly still here, rampant among us. It's not over yet. This battle must come to an apex, and the Saint's blood avenged.

I had a dream of the rapture, after the first of the recent four blood moons, in 2014. Within the next two months I had five successive visions, about current events and the book of Revelation. These visions would not leave me till I started writing them down. I felt a strong urge to share what God has given to me. Through His visions given me, and as I was writing this book, the Lord revealed to me the true meaning of the entire book of Revelation.

The first vision was of all the present evil going on in the world today, and how it pertains scripturally, to the book of Revelation, and the true believers. It is all written in this book.

The second vision was to let me know Jesus is coming for his Bride, those who love his appearing, very soon. So in prayer I sought the Lord as to what I myself might need to change, and was told to pray, "Lord, let me walk in the paths of old." I was awoken the next day with a strong desire to worship, and hearing the words, "Your calendars are perverted." I was led on a study of the true worship days of God, and how Satan has stolen His true appointed worship days. I have explained it in the chapter "God's Appointed Worship Day."

The third vision was of a Polar Shift Reversal in the Earth's atmosphere that will change our lives forever. This Polar Shift Reversal is explained later in this book. This was a dramatic vision, which drew me to really want to share this information divinely given to me, for now is the appointed time.

The fourth vision was to tell me that this present evil and Polar Shift Reversal event, will lead to the Abomination of Desolation, spoken of in the Book of Daniel. So I also did a deep study of Daniel, to verify, written in chapter 14.

The fifth vision purposed to reveal that this red Planet X, some people have been talking about, is the Red Dragon seen in the sky, in the book of Revelation. I will explain all I saw and learned from God in this book.

2. JOHN'S REVELATION TO THE CHURCHES

Let us take the time to go through the entire book of Revelation, and juxtapose the visions, and understandings given to me, by the Lord, to help clarify the book of Revelation. Be patient the unveiling gets more intense as we progress through unlocking God's secrets.

> ***REV 1:*** **KJV**
>
> *1) The Revelation of Jesus Christ, which God gave unto him, to show unto his servants' things which must shortly come to pass; and he sent and signified it by his angel unto his servant John:*
>
> *2) Who bare record of the word of God, and of the testimony of Jesus Christ, and of all things that he saw.*
>
> *3) Blessed is he that readeth, and they that hear the words of this prophecy, and keep those things which are written therein: for the time is at hand.*

Meaning: The angel of the Lord told John this book was meant to be shut up, and to only be revealed when; the direct time is at hand. These scriptures have been reviewed and interpreted confusingly many times, by the best scholars, but God only in His perfect time reveals it, to his simple servants, and prophets. So if we can only now understand, then the time is at hand.

It was not to be revealed till the end, when Jesus is coming, the battle is at hand, and there is a very short time left.

The Seven Churches: God's Last Plea

REV 1:

4) John to the seven churches which are in Asia: Grace be unto you, and peace, from Him which is, and which was, and which is to come; and from the seven Spirits which are before his throne;

5) And from Jesus Christ, who is the faithful witness, and the first begotten of the dead, and the prince of the kings of the earth. Unto him that loved us, and washed us from our sins in his own blood,

6) And hath made us kings and priests unto God and his Father; to him be glory and dominion for ever and ever. Amen.

Meaning: These Churches were in Asia, not in Israel, and written by John's perspective, a Jew, that meant the world outside of Israel, or to all of us. This is symbolizing the whole known world, and the #7 is meaning completion.

From the beginning and the end or God, Jesus, and the seven Spirits of God, (Faith, Hope, Love, Peace, Mercy,

Righteousness, and Truth), sounds like, a message from the Father, Son, and Holy Spirit, with a purpose, to a final end.

> ***REV 1:***
>
> *7) Behold, he cometh with clouds; and every eye shall see him, and they also which pierced him: and all kindreds of the earth shall wail because of him. Even so, Amen.*
>
> ***8)** I am Alpha and Omega, the beginning and the ending, saith the Lord, which is, and which was, and which is to come, the Almighty.*
>
> ***9)** I John, who also am your brother, and companion in tribulation, and in the kingdom and patience of Jesus Christ, was in the isle that is called Patmos, for the word of God, and for the testimony of Jesus Christ.*
>
> ***10)** I was in the Spirit on the Lord's day, and heard behind me a great voice, as of a trumpet,*
>
> ***11)** Saying, I am Alpha and Omega, the first and the last: and, What thou seest, write in a book, and send it unto the seven churches which are in Asia; unto Ephesus, and unto Smyrna, and unto Pergamos, and unto Thyatira, and unto Sardis, and unto Philadelphia, and unto Laodicea.*

This refers to the second coming of Jesus, at the end of time. That's when all creation will behold Him. John has to write what he sees and send it to the Churches.

Now here is a real clue; John was out of body, and on the Lords Day, or the Sabbath day, hearing the sound of a trumpet.

This is sort of like being present in the scene of Christ's second coming.

Matt 24:20-21, or Mark 13:18, refers to, praying that your flight will not be in the winter or Sabbath day, for then will be a great Tribulation. So, I feel the rapture, and second coming is on Gods appointed Sabbath Day, and not our Sunday. We should make an effort to find out when the appointed days are. I will talk of this at the end of this book, in Chapter 18.

Interestingly, New Moons are not Sabbath Days, but often Full Moons are.

> ***REV 1:***
>
> ***12)*** *And I turned to see the voice that spake with me. And being turned, I saw seven golden candlesticks;*
>
> ***13)*** *And in the midst of the seven candlesticks one like unto the Son of man, clothed with a garment down to the foot, and girt about the paps with a golden girdle.*
>
> ***14)*** *His head and his hairs were white like wool, as white as snow; and his eyes were as a flame of fire;*
>
> ***15)*** *And his feet like unto fine brass, as if they burned in a furnace; and his voice as the sound of many waters.*
>
> ***16)*** *And he had in his right hand seven stars: and out of his mouth went a sharp two edged sword: and his countenance was as the sun shineth in his strength.*

> ***17)*** *And when I saw him, I fell at his feet as dead. And he laid his right hand upon me, saying unto me, Fear not; I am the first and the last:*
>
> ***18)*** *I am he that liveth, and was dead; and, behold, I am alive for evermore, Amen; and have the keys of hell and of death.*
>
> ***19)*** *Write the things which thou hast seen, and the things which are, and the things which shall be hereafter;*
>
> ***20)*** *The mystery of the seven stars which thou sawest in my right hand, and the seven golden candlesticks. The seven stars are the angels of the seven churches: and the seven candlesticks which thou sawest are the seven churches.*

Jesus is the Light among all these candles, walking to and fro amongst us, and clothed with the vesture of God. He is the full story, and holds all the answers and keys.

Daniel describes a similar incident, and sees Jesus lit bright, in the same way, in the book of Daniel, chapter 10. The sound of many waters could be the many souls raptured with Him.

There is a Guardian for each church, depicted by the seven stars.

> ***REV 2:***
>
> ***1)*** *Unto the angel of the church of* ***Ephesus*** *write; These things saith he that holdeth the seven stars in his right hand, who walketh in the midst of the seven golden candlesticks;*
>
> ***2)*** *I know thy works, and thy labour, and thy patience, and how thou canst not bear them which*

> *are evil: and thou hast tried them which say they are apostles, and are not, and hast found them liars:*
>
> ***3)*** *And hast borne, and hast patience, and for my name's sake hast laboured, and hast not fainted.*
>
> ***4)*** *Nevertheless I have somewhat against thee, because thou hast left thy first love.*
>
> ***5)*** *Remember therefore from whence thou art fallen, and repent, and do the first works; or else I will come unto thee quickly, and will remove thy candlestick out of his place, except thou repent.*
>
> ***6)*** *But this thou hast, that thou hatest the deeds of the Nicolaitans, which I also hate.*
>
> *7) He that hath an ear, let him hear what the Spirit saith unto the churches; To him that overcometh will I give to eat of the tree of life, which is in the midst of the paradise of God.*

This Church seems to have a lot on the ball, but has overdone the works for the Church, doing it their own way. They are too busy, so much so that they forgot, to spend precious time with their first Love, Jesus, the reason for it all. He warns us to overcome this.

In Matthew 25, Jesus shuts some out and says, "Be gone I never Knew you." We are saved by grace and not by good works so no one can boast.

REV 2:

8) *And unto the angel of the church in* ***Smyrna*** *write; These things saith the first and the last, which was dead, and is alive;*

9) *I know thy works, and tribulation, and poverty, (but thou art rich) and I know the blasphemy of them which say they are Jews, and are not, but are the synagogue of Satan.*

10) *Fear none of those things which thou shalt suffer: behold, the devil shall cast some of you into prison, that ye may be tried; and ye shall have tribulation ten days: be thou faithful unto death, and I will give thee a crown of life.*

11) *He that hath an ear, let him hear what the Spirit saith unto the churches; He that overcometh shall not be hurt of the second death.*

These are they that will have to go through much suffering, hunger, and poverty, maybe even death. He encourages them to not be afraid, stand strong and He will crown them.

REV 2:

12) *And to the angel of the church in* ***Pergamos*** *write; These things saith he which hath the sharp sword with two edges;*

13) *I know thy works, and where thou dwellest, even where Satan's seat is: and thou holdest fast my name, and hast not denied my faith, even in those days wherein Antipas was my faithful martyr, who was slain among you, where Satan dwelleth.*

***14)** But I have a few things against thee, because thou hast there them that hold the doctrine of Balaam, who taught Balac to cast a stumbling block before the children of Israel, to eat things sacrificed unto idols, and to commit fornication.*

***15)** So hast thou also them that hold the doctrine of the Nicolaitans, which thing I hate.*

***16)** Repent; or else I will come unto thee quickly, and will fight against them with the sword of my mouth.*

***17)** He that hath an ear, let him hear what the Spirit saith unto the churches; To him that overcometh will I give to eat of the hidden manna, and will give him a white stone, and in the stone a new name written, which no man knoweth saving he that receiveth it.*

These dwell among Satan's people, but they love God. He says they have bad teachings and are ingesting poisons. They need to repent, and come out, or they too will be under His wrath and sword. But if they overcome, he will give them his hidden manna, or truths to free them.

REV 2:

***18)** And unto the angel of the church in **Thyatira** write; These things saith the Son of God, who hath his eyes like unto a flame of fire, and his feet are like fine brass;*

***19)** I know thy works, and charity, and service, and faith, and thy patience, and thy works; and the last to be more than the first.*

20) *Notwithstanding I have a few things against thee, because thou sufferest that woman Jezebel, which calleth herself a prophetess, to teach and to seduce my servants to commit fornication, and to eat things sacrificed unto idols.*

21) *And I gave her space to repent of her fornication; and she repented not.*

22) *Behold, I will cast her into a bed, and them that commit adultery with her into great tribulation, except they repent of their deeds.*

23) *And I will kill her children with death; and all the churches shall know that I am he which searcheth the reins and hearts: and I will give unto every one of you according to your works.*

24) *But unto you I say, and unto the rest in Thyatira, as many as have not this doctrine, and which have not known the depths of Satan, as they speak; I will put upon you none other burden.*

25) *But that which ye have already hold fast till I come.*

26) *And he that overcometh, and keepeth my works unto the end, to him will I give power over the nations:*

27) *And he shall rule them with a rod of iron; as the vessels of a potter shall they be broken to shivers: even as I received of my Father.*

28) *And I will give him the morning star.*

29) *He that hath an ear, let him hear what the Spirit saith unto the churches.*

This Church speaks both truth, and also as the world, and are works driven. Jesus is searching the heart.

Being driven by works is subtly a type of Pride, and is one of the greatest attacks to overcome. The Great Deception can also be self-worship, and those who will not repent will go through the Great Tribulation. Overcomers of a greater fight will receive a greater reward, to shine as a star forever.

Terms like Jezebel, Baal, Balaam, Balac, Synagog of Satan, Nicolaitans, all have to do with perverting our children, changing our DNA, sacrifices to gods, subliminal deceptions, and the like. This is a book in itself, and not the purpose here. This was a problem back in John's day, and we still very much have the problem today. People in high places are more often locked in fraternities, giving allegiances to Grand Masters, compromising the faith, and allegiance. They pay this price for the fame and wealth of the world. This is what God calls being defiled with woman, or other gods.

REV 3:

1) And unto the angel of the church in ***Sardis*** *write; These things saith he that hath the seven Spirits of God, and the seven stars; I know thy works, that thou hast a name that thou livest, and art dead.*

2) Be watchful, and strengthen the things which remain, that are ready to die: for I have not found thy works perfect before God.

3) Remember therefore how thou hast received and heard, and hold fast, and repent. If therefore thou shalt not watch, I will come on thee as a thief, and thou shalt not know what hour I will come upon thee.

__4__) Thou hast a few names even in Sardis which have not defiled their garments; and they shall walk with me in white: for they are worthy.

__5__) He that overcometh, the same shall be clothed in white raiment; and I will not blot out his name out of the book of life, but I will confess his name before my Father, and before his angels.

__6__) He that hath an ear, let him hear what the Spirit saith unto the churches.

This is what we call the dead Church. They do the least bit expected of them. He says remember back when you were excited for Christ, if you do not, your name could be rubbed out.

REV 3:

7) And to the angel of the church in __Philadelphia__ write; These things saith he that is holy, he that is true, he that hath the key of David, he that openeth, and no man shutteth; and shutteth, and no man openeth;

__8__) I know thy works: behold, I have set before thee an open door, and no man can shut it: for thou hast a little strength, and hast kept my word, and hast not denied my name.

__9__) Behold, I will make them of the synagogue of Satan, which say they are Jews, and are not, but do lie; behold, I will make them to come and worship before thy feet, and to know that I have loved thee.

__10__) Because thou hast kept the word of my patience, I also will keep thee from the hour of temptation,

> *which shall come upon all the world, to try them that dwell upon the earth.*
>
> ***11)*** *Behold, I come quickly: hold that fast which thou hast, that no man take thy crown.*
>
> ***12)*** *Him that overcometh will I make a pillar in the temple of my God, and he shall go no more out: and I will write upon him the name of my God, and the name of the city of my God, which is new Jerusalem, which cometh down out of heaven from my God: and I will write upon him my new name.*
>
> ***13)*** *He that hath an ear, let him hear what the Spirit saith unto the churches.*

This Church has overcome some temptations already, and have not compromised the truth. They have favor and the love of God. If they can hold on till the end, they will most likely be the Bride of Christ, and be sealed, carrying His new Name.

> ***REV 3:***
>
> ***14)*** *And unto the angel of the church of the* ***Laodiceans*** *write; These things saith the Amen, the faithful and true witness, the beginning of the creation of God;*
>
> ***15)*** *I know thy works, that thou art neither cold nor hot: I would thou wert cold or hot.*
>
> ***16)*** *So then because thou art lukewarm, and neither cold nor hot, I will spue thee out of my mouth.*
>
> ***17)*** *Because thou sayest, I am rich, and increased with goods, and have need of nothing; and knowest not that thou art wretched, and miserable, and poor, and blind, and naked:*

> ***18)*** *I counsel thee to buy of me gold tried in the fire, that thou mayest be rich; and white raiment, that thou mayest be clothed, and that the shame of thy nakedness do not appear; and anoint thine eyes with eyesalve, that thou mayest see.*
>
> ***19)*** *As many as I love, I rebuke and chasten: be zealous therefore, and repent.*
>
> ***20)*** *** Behold, I stand at the door, and knock: if any man hear my voice, and open the door,* ***I will come in to him****, and will sup with him, and he with me.*
>
> ***21)*** *To him that overcometh will I grant to sit with me in my throne, even as I also overcame, and am set down with my Father in his throne.*
>
> ***22)*** *He that hath an ear, let him hear what the Spirit saith unto the churches.*

This Church is lukewarm, and well to do, so they don't think they need Jesus much. They have no need of anything, and don't feel anything will ever hurt them. Many times God tried to wake them up and show them they are in danger, but they would not listen. He wants them to wake up and be zealous for Jesus. Most are not saved yet. But in verse 20 Jesus pleads with them to come to Him, to be saved, and have power to overcome.

More than likely they will be left behind, to be tested and forced to choose their God, with one last chance to repent.

REV 4:

1) *After this I looked, and, behold, a door was opened in heaven: and the first voice which I heard was as it were of a trumpet talking with me; which said, Come up hither, and I will show thee things which must be* <u>*hereafter.*</u>

2) *And immediately I was in the spirit: and, behold, a throne was set in heaven, and one sat on the throne.*

3) *And he that sat was to look upon like a jasper and a sardine stone: and there was a rainbow round about the throne, in sight like unto an emerald.*

4) *And round about the throne were four and twenty seats: and upon the seats I saw four and twenty elders sitting, clothed in white raiment; and they had on their heads crowns of gold.*

5) *And out of the throne proceeded lightnings and thunderings and voices: and there were seven lamps of fire burning before the throne, which are the seven Spirits of God.*

6) *And before the throne there was a sea of glass like unto crystal: and in the midst of the throne, and round about the throne, were four beasts full of eyes before and behind.*

7) *And the first beast was like a lion, and the second beast like a calf, and the third beast had a face as a man, and the fourth beast was like a flying eagle.*

8) *And the four beasts had each of them six wings about him; and they were full of eyes within: and they rest not day and night, saying,* <u>**Holy, holy,**</u>

> ***holy***, *Lord God Almighty, which was, and is, and is to come.*
>
> ***9)*** *And when those beasts give glory and honour and thanks to him that sat on the throne, who liveth for ever and ever,*
>
> ***10)*** *The four and twenty elders fall down before him that sat on the throne, and worship him that liveth for ever and ever, and cast their crowns before the throne, saying,*
>
> ***11)*** *Thou art worthy, O Lord, to receive glory and honour and power: for thou hast created all things, and for thy pleasure they are and were created.*

Repeating something three times establishes the importance, and agrees Father Son, and Holy Ghost. This shows God's just judgments. All give Glory to God in Heaven.

Now is a new final season started: A season of the *Bridegroom coming*, and final battle to do away with all evil. Satan would try to keep the Church blinded to God's last new season, by fooling them into staying in a perpetual Prosperity, and Building Season. Satan will use the scriptures to keep them there. Because the Word is true, God wants us to prosper, Satan will create a conflict with the true events of Jesus and God, forgetting there is a timing and season to everything.

Satan purposes to change times, which can deceive even the Elect. Be led by the Holy Spirit in all, to protect yourself, and know God's true season. What profits a man if he builds in the wrong season, all will come to naught, so catch up. Ecclesiastes 3:1–11 states, "To everything *there is* a season, and a time to every purpose under the heaven:…a time to break down, and a time to build up; a time of war, and a time of peace."

REV 5:

1) *And I saw in the right hand of him that sat on the throne a book written within and on the backside, sealed with seven seals.*

2) *And I saw a strong angel proclaiming with a loud voice, Who is worthy to open the book, and to loose the seals thereof?*

3) *And no man in heaven, nor in earth, neither under the earth, was able to open the book, neither to look thereon.*

4) *And I wept much, because no man was found worthy to open and to read the book, neither to look thereon.*

5) *And one of the elders saith unto me, Weep not: behold, the Lion of the tribe of Judah, the Root of David, hath prevailed to open the book, and to loose the seven seals thereof.*

6) *And I beheld, and, lo, in the midst of the throne and of the four beasts, and in the midst of the elders, stood a Lamb as it had been slain, having seven horns and seven eyes, which are the seven Spirits of God sent forth into all the earth.*

A prophetic scroll of God's final righteous judgment plan to do away with all evil is in God's right hand. This scroll is written on both sides and sealed as it is scrolled up in seven sections. Each chapter is sealed so as one could see only a part at a time.

Jesus was the only one with the legal right to open and see the eternal plans of God, and share it with us.

REV 5:

7) And he came and took the book out of the right hand of him that sat upon the throne.

***8)** And when he had taken the book, the four beasts and four and twenty elders fell down before the Lamb, having every one of them harps, and golden vials full of odours, which are the prayers of saints.*

***9)** And they sung a new song, saying, Thou art worthy to take the book, and to open the seals thereof: for thou wast slain, and hast redeemed us to God by thy blood out of every kindred, and tongue, and people, and nation;*

***10)** And hast made us unto our God kings and priests: and we shall reign on the earth.*

***11)** And I beheld, and I heard the voice of many angels round about the throne and the beasts and the elders: and the number of them was ten thousand times ten thousand, and thousands of thousands; (over 110 Million)*

***12)** Saying with a loud voice, Worthy is the Lamb that was slain to receive power, and riches, and wisdom, and strength, and honour, and glory, and blessing.*

***13)** And every creature which is in heaven, and on the earth, and under the earth, and such as are in the sea, and all that are in them, heard I saying, Blessing, and honour, and glory, and power, be unto him that sitteth upon the throne, and unto the Lamb for ever and ever.*

> ***14)*** *And the four beasts said, Amen. And the four and twenty elders fell down and worshipped him that liveth for ever and ever.*

Jesus is endowed with seven more gifts of rewards that He may share with those, that overcome.

3. THE SEVEN SEALS

"Come and See"

The Seven Seals are the *unveilings* of all that is to come. It is a Showing of what is going on, and the last seal, shows the full future, all trumps, all vials of wrath, the judgment, the new Heaven, the new Earth, and the New Jerusalem, the Bride.

The four beasts are somehow related to the first four seals.

The seven Trumps are warnings of God, of what will happen when <u>God takes His protection away.</u> Two witnesses of God are present at this time.

The seven Angels with bowls are the final Wrath of God (without the Spirit of God present).

REV 6: New World Order

1) *And I saw when the Lamb opened* ***<u>one</u>*** *of the seals, and I heard, as it were the noise of thunder, one of the four <u>beasts</u> saying, <u>Come and see</u>.*

2) *And I saw, and behold a white horse: and he that sat on him had a bow; and a crown was given unto him: and he went forth conquering, and to conquer.*

ONE WORLD RELIGION Rising: A religious entity given a crown of power. This purity masquerader has the power to kill in his hand. In time, at the last, all will be asked to convert or die.

REV 6:

*3) And when he had opened the **second seal**, I heard the second beast say, Come and see.*

***4)** And there went out another horse that was red: and power was given to him that sat thereon to take peace from the earth, and that they should kill one another: and there was given unto him a great sword.*

ONE WORLD GOVERNMENT Rising: This is a forcible peace. "Many will be killed in the name of peace." More than likely Communist Russia is involved with enforcing it.

REV 6:

*5) And when he had opened the **third seal**, I heard the third beast say, Come and see. And I beheld, and lo a black horse; and he that sat on him had a pair of balances in his hand.*

***6)** And I heard a voice in the midst of the four beasts say, a measure of wheat for a penny, and three measures of barley for a penny; and see thou hurt not the oil and the wine.*

ONE WORLD CURRENCY and TRADE Rising: This will set up the mark of the Beast. Food will be very scarce, and may be in controlled rationing. There is a control of oil, and they are drunk with the whore's wine. It will set all countries' accounting books back in the black.

REV 6:

7) *And when he had opened the* ***fourth seal****, I heard the voice of the fourth beast say, Come and see.*

8) *And I looked, and behold a pale horse: and his name that sat on him was Death, and Hell followed with him. And power was given unto them over the fourth part of the earth, to kill with sword, and with hunger, and with death, and with the beasts of the earth.*

ONE WORLD MILITARY REGIMENT Rising: Rough controlling *martial law*, and One World *Policing*. This is a very powerful and absolute uncompromised control. Many will die. Soldiers are taking orders from the Destroyer, Apollyon, as in Hitler's day.

REV 6:

9) *And when he had opened the* ***fifth seal****, I saw under the altar the souls of them that were slain for the word of God, and for the testimony which they held:*

10) *And they cried with a loud voice, saying, How long, O Lord, holy and true, dost thou not judge and avenge our blood on them that dwell on the earth?*

11) *And white robes were given unto every one of them; and it was said unto them, that they should rest yet for a little season, until their fellow* *servants also and their brethren, that should be killed as they were, should be fulfilled.*

These are as the Dead in Christ: Probably those who are ready to be raptured first, signifying a spiritual death to this world. Often when Jesus was talking of physically dead, He said: "She sleepeth," like in Matthew 9:24, "He said unto them, give place: for the maid is not dead, but sleepeth. And they laughed him to scorn." Also in Mark 5:39, John 11:11, 1 Kings 1:21, etc.

He used the word dead when He was talking of the spiritual dead to this world, like in; Luke 9:60, Ephesians 5:14, and Colossians 2:20: "Therefore if you be dead with Christ from the rudiments of the world, why, as though living in the world, are you subject to ordinances." Also in Romans 6:8: "Now if we are dead with Christ, we believe that we shall also live with him."

WARNING: This passage could easily be speaking of an energy blackout, by a solar flare from the sun, or a manmade microwave event, putting us in darkness seeking God intensely before Jesus comes. This event would turn off all electronics, and communication for all, from three to forty-five days. God did speak to me of a short time in darkness. I feel it is before the Polar shift and could be at this event.

REV 6:

*12) And I beheld when he had opened the **sixth seal**, and, lo, there was a great earthquake; and the sun became black as sackcloth of hair, and the moon became as blood;*

> ***13)*** *And the stars of heaven fell unto the earth, even as a fig tree casteth her untimely figs, when she is shaken of a mighty wind.*
>
> ***14)*** *And the heaven departed as a scroll when it is rolled together; and every mountain and island were moved out of their places.*
>
> ***15)*** *And the kings of the earth, and the great men, and the rich men, and the chief captains, and the mighty men, and every bondman, and every free man, hid themselves in the dens and in the rocks of the mountains;*
>
> ***16)*** *And said to the mountains and rocks, Fall on us, and hide us from the face of him that sitteth on the throne, and from the wrath of the Lamb:*
>
> ***17)*** *For the great day of his wrath is come; and who shall be able to stand?*

My morning vision: I saw a planet come between the Earth and the Sun. It was very large so as to cover the whole Sun, and this caused the moon to become red. The Earth was quaking all over, all people fell and could not stand up, like no quake has ever been. The Earth's poles shifted, down side up, a total flip. The stars seem to roll around the Earth in the sky, as if to form a tunnel, but I knew it was the Earth rolling. The wind was strong, and a few large and small boulders drawn from this planet, fell to the Earth, along with red sand. Governments, and everyone in high places, and the rich, ran to find their bunkers, but everyone else did not do as well, having no place to go. Large rogue waves flooded all the shores.

It is impossible to have both a solar and a lunar eclipse at the same time. The moon must be lined up with the Sun on one side of the Earth or the other, unless there is another body causing the Sun to eclipse.

In a polar reversal, every continent and island would be displaced on our present maps, moved out of their place.

NASA scientists have been observing a red iron oxide planet, with cloud wings and a tail of debris, which has been headed to our solar system for fifty years. Many scientists have tried to tell us, but it was always suppressed.

1/30/1983

The New York Times

Ideas & Trends

Continued

Clues Get Warm in the Search for Planet X

Was written in *New York Times* 1983.

The Red Planet Is the Dragon

In my fifth morning vision, I saw this red planet, with two debris wings, in the sky, and it turned into a Red Dragon. The Lord told me this planet is the great red dragon seen in the sky, of Revelation 12:3.

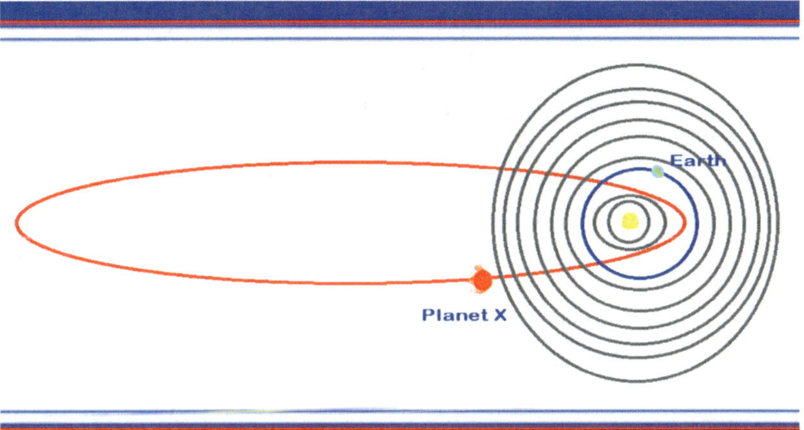

Navy Astronomer estimate a long elliptical path of observed Planet X orbit.

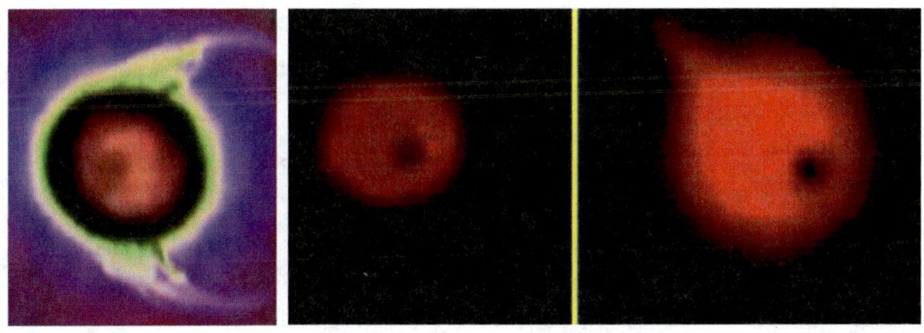

2003 infrared lens telescope finds wings

DNIr4808n Comparing 2008 with 2012. (simulations)
NEMESIS: Also found Planet X, Jan 10, 2014

This planet, called Planet X, is crossing our path soon, and it is very real. (You should look it up for yourself.) This planet probably has seven moons about it. It is said to be seven times Earth's size. It could easily eclipse our Sun, and is so highly magnetic. Planet X was said to have flipped several planets along the way and caused havoc. It drags a lot of debris, because it is highly magnetic, with red iron oxide.

Many secret brotherhood fraternities, like Masons, and other names, have been tracking this planet's orbit, approaching closer to Earth for over fifty years. And yes, the Pope in Rome is one of the trackers. He has his own observatory, and this news is probably the last prediction, of the Fatima children. The Observatory is one of the oldest astronomical research institutions in the world. Its headquarters are at the Pope's summer residence in Castel Gandolfo, just outside of Rome.

Planet X is very close now, and as we cross the red planet's tail it is causing our Earth to quake, make loud moaning or horn sounds, red rain, red rivers, hail ice balls, hail fireballs, causing more fires, volcanoes, the large meteor in Russia in February 2013, and yes, we have four poles now, two in the north and two in the south.

We now have seen Fireballs.

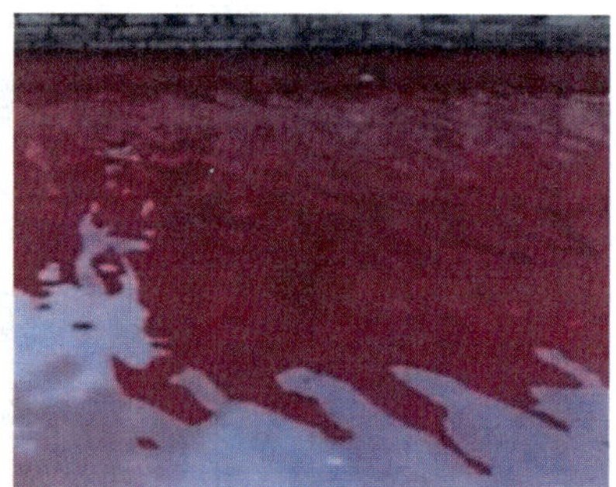

Blood Rivers are seen in various global areas.

In July 2001, South India had two months of red rain. Dr. Godfrey Louis did a study on the red rain and found live blood cells of unknown or no DNA. In 2012 and 2013, a flood of red rivers appeared all around the world, such as the Yangtze River and others.

The book *ZENITH 2016*, by Thomas Horn, is an expositive study of what these secret societies have learned, and don't want us to know. They in essence have placed Planet X's coming in 2016. In fact, they are celebrating its coming, heralding it as the great coming of Satan. In the thirty-second degree level, some Masons are told a secret, that Jesus's real name was Satan, and some jargon of why. Many are falling for it. I say thank God for the Holy Spirit, our teacher. But remember, they also have a counterfeit spirit.

The island of Malta has great ancient architecture depicting this red-winged planet boldly on their buildings, and the coming eclipse, heralding the second coming of Satan.

Ball-size hail, fell in Texas April 3, 2014.

Worldwide photos of two suns, 2014

4. BEFORE THE QUAKE

The Four Angels

REV 7:

1) *And after these things I saw four angels standing on the four corners of the earth, holding the four winds of the earth, that the wind should not blow on the earth, nor on the sea, nor on any tree.*

2) *And I saw another angel ascending from the east, having the seal of the living God: and he cried with a loud voice to the four angels, to whom it was given to hurt the earth and the sea,*

3) *Saying, Hurt not the earth, neither the sea, nor the trees, till we have sealed the servants of our God in their foreheads.*

4) *And I heard the number of them which were sealed: and there were sealed an hundred and forty and four thousand of all the tribes of the children of Israel.*

5) *Of the tribe of Juda were sealed twelve thousand. Of the tribe of Reuben were sealed*

> *twelve thousand. Of the tribe of Gad were sealed twelve thousand.*
>
> ***6)*** *Of the tribe of Aser were sealed twelve thousand. Of the tribe of Nepthalim were sealed twelve thousand. Of the tribe of Manasses were sealed twelve thousand.*
>
> ***7)*** *Of the tribe of Simeon were sealed twelve thousand. Of the tribe of Levi were sealed twelve thousand. Of the tribe of Issachar were sealed twelve thousand.*
>
> ***8)*** *Of the tribe of Zabulon were sealed twelve thousand. Of the tribe of Joseph were sealed twelve thousand. Of the tribe of Benjamin were sealed twelve thousand.*

These four corners of the Earth are the four poles we have now. Four angels are sent to keep the poles in place long enough to seal Christ's Bride. There will be a great wind coming that will literally hurt the earth and seas, tsunamis all over the world. In October 2009, pole arches changed. In 2010, two poles on the north emerged, and in 2012 it got worse, we now have four poles. Now there is a breach in the magnetic field the size of a planet.

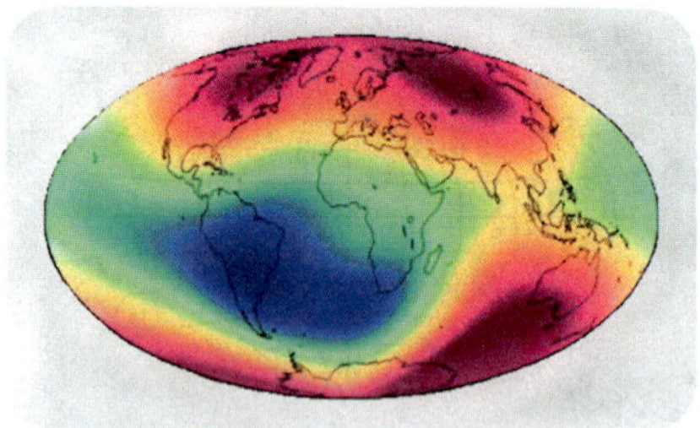

We now have four poles 6-30-2014.

Tracking the last ten years of pole movement.

By now you must realize that 144,000 are not many people. These are to be sealed by the angels ready to escape what is about to happen. Because the dead in Christ will rise first. Any way you look at it, these select are distinct.

I have come to know that the dead in Christ are not those buried in the ground, but those who die to this world, reaching all the way in Christ. His spotless Bride, ready for His coming. So this 144,000 may not necessarily be only the Jews we know. We were grafted in. Above, it said,

> "Behold, I will make them of the synagogue of Satan, which say they are Jews, and are not, but do lie; behold, I will make them to come and worship before thy feet, and to know that I have loved thee." **(Rev 3:9)**
>
> "Therefore if you be dead with Christ from the rudiments of the world, why, as though living in the world, are you subject to ordinances." **(Col 2:20)**
>
> "Now if we died with Christ, we believe that we will…" **(Rom 6:8)**

REV 7:

9) *After this I beheld, and, lo, a great multitude, which no man could number, of all nations, and kindreds, and people, and tongues, stood before the throne, and before the Lamb, clothed with white robes, and palms in their hands;*

10) *And cried with a loud voice, saying, Salvation to our God which sitteth upon the throne, and unto the Lamb.*

> ***11)*** *And all the angels stood round about the throne, and about the elders and the four beasts, and fell before the throne on their faces, and worshipped God,*
>
> ***12)*** *Saying, Amen: Blessing, and glory, and wisdom, and thanksgiving, and honour, and power, and might, be unto our God for ever and ever. Amen.*
>
> ***13)*** *And one of the elders answered, saying unto me, What are these which are arrayed in white robes? and whence came they?*
>
> ***14)*** *And I said unto him, Sir, thou knowest. And he said to me, These are they which came out of great tribulation, and have washed their robes, and made them white in the blood of the Lamb.*
>
> ***15)*** *Therefore are they before the throne of God, and serve him day and night in his temple: and he that sitteth on the throne shall dwell among them.*
>
> ***16)*** *They shall hunger no more, neither thirst anymore; neither shall the sun light on them, nor any heat.*
>
> ***17)*** *For the Lamb which is in the midst of the throne shall feed them, and shall lead them unto living fountains of waters: and God shall wipe away all tears from their eyes.*

This means a great multitude, or millions, of other believers, who died through the polar reversal effect on the earth, tsunamis, earthquakes, falling debris, and winds. These were redeemed by the blood of Christ, and they were not left to go through any further Tribulation. Understand that both the 144,000 raptured Bride, and this great multitude event, are almost one on top of the other. The hosts of Heaven welcome them.

Yes, there will be many left behind, but don't count all as lost yet. Those left will have a chance to prove themselves, and if they can overcome they will receive a crown for it, at Jesus's final coming, but their trials will not be pleasant.

5. THIS IS HOW ALL WILL UNFOLD TO THE END: THE SEVENTH SEAL

The seventh seal is equal to the Rest to be unveiled.

REV 8:

1) *And when he had opened the* ***seventh seal****, there was silence in heaven about the space of* ***half an hour.***

2) *And I saw the seven angels which stood before God; and to them were given seven trumpets.*

3) *And another angel came and stood at the altar, having a golden censer; and there was given unto him much incense, that he should offer it with the prayers of all saints upon the golden altar which was before the throne.*

4) *And the smoke of the incense, which came with the prayers of the saints, ascended up before God out of the angel's hand.*

5) *And the angel took the censer, and filled it with fire of the altar, and cast it into the earth: and there were voices, and thunderings, and lightnings, and an earthquake.*

> ***6)*** *And the seven angels which had the seven trumpets prepared themselves to sound.*

Yes, this is the same earthquake that just happened in the polar reversal. The author is bringing us back a bit, to continue the story on and make us understand there are angels getting ready to sound seven alarms, at this time. So again, <u>come and see</u> how it happens, before the real wake up call.

The prayers of the saints are very important at this point. It may save many left behind to be strong and overcome.

Here is a big clue: Last time we started where the angels were holding back the four poles. Well, they bought us half an hour. This is when the First Fruits to Christ are sealed, ready to be raptured.

Let me show to you how this half hour of silence in heaven can work. Scientists have proven that in the last ten years, the earth has been slowing its speed of rotation, about an inch a year. So much so that they are now setting up to give us a Leap Hour, every so often. This change is something that has never happened before. So it is not hard to believe the earth could actually <u>stand still for half hour</u> before the great event. The whole face of the Earth, and life as we have come to know it, will forever change. We are about to be thrown into a parallel universe, of the dark side, without the Spirit of God's restraint. The Twilight Zone.

> ***REV 8:***
>
> *7) The* ***<u>first angel sounded</u>****, and there followed hail and fire mingled with blood, and they were cast upon the earth: and the third part of trees was burnt up, and all green grass was burnt up.*

8) *And the* ***second angel sounded****, and as it were a great mountain burning with fire was cast into the sea: and the third part of the sea became blood;*

(Burning Meteor) Right foot of Angel, Rev. 10:2

9) *And the third part of the creatures which were in the sea, and had life, died; and the third part of the ships were destroyed.*

10) *And the* ***third angel sounded****, and there fell a great star from heaven, burning as it were a lamp, and it fell upon the third part of the rivers, and upon the fountains of waters;*

Left foot of Angel, Rev. 10:2

11) And the name of the star is called ***Wormwood:*** *and the third part of the waters became wormwood; and many men died of the waters, because they were made bitter.*

12) *And the* ***fourth angel sounded****, and the third part of the sun was smitten, and the third part of the moon, and the third part of the stars; so as the third part of them was darkened, and the day shone not for a third part of it, and the night likewise.*

13) *And I beheld, and heard an angel flying through the midst of heaven, saying with a loud voice,* ***Woe, woe, woe,*** *to the inhabiters of the earth by reason of the other voices of the trumpet of the three angels, which are yet to sound!*

This red Planet X has already brought us some hail fireballs at certain times of year. We have more fires than in all our history. There will certainly be many fires when that day comes. The dust off this planet will cause the waters to seem as blood, and is chemically very unhealthy for us. Many animals will die in the water, and it will be undrinkable. The heavy magnetic pull will cause our crust to break up, and the volcanoes to blow.

There soon will be larger asteroids hitting the earth from the debris clouds around this Planet X. Good drinking water will be very scarce, and food also. The sun may also be too close at this time to Planet X, and pull one of its moons out of orbit, to itself. If anything large hits the sun it will cause solar flares, and the Earth will go into darkness for a while.

I feel these first four events will be in close succession. *Wormwood* means destruction and bitterness.

Three Wows are very urgent warnings, coming to the root of what God is trying to say to these left on Earth: This is your last chance to repent, and change.

REV 9:

1) *And the* ***fifth angel sounded****, and I saw a star fall from heaven unto the earth: and to him was given the key of the bottomless pit.*

2) *And he opened the bottomless pit; and there arose a smoke out of the pit, as the smoke of a great furnace; and the sun and the air were darkened by reason of the smoke of the pit.*

3) *And there came out of the smoke locusts upon the earth: and unto them was given power, as the scorpions of the earth have power.*

4) *And it was commanded them that they should not hurt the grass of the earth, neither any green thing, neither any tree; but only those men which have not the seal of God in their foreheads.*

> ***5)*** *And to them it was given that they should not kill them, but that they should be tormented five months: and their torment was as the torment of a scorpion, when he striketh a man.*
>
> ***6)*** *And in those days shall men seek death, and shall not find it; and shall desire to die, and death shall flee from them.*
>
> *7) And the shapes of the locusts were like unto horses prepared unto battle; and on their heads were as it were crowns like gold, and their faces were as the faces of men.*
>
> ***8)*** *And they had hair as the hair of women, and their teeth were as the teeth of lions.*
>
> ***9)*** *And they had breastplates, as it were breastplates of iron; and the sound of their wings was as the sound of chariots of many horses running to battle.*
>
> ***10)*** *And they had tails like unto scorpions, and there were stings in their tails: and their power was to hurt men five months.*
>
> ***11)*** *And they had a king over them, which is the angel of the bottomless pit, whose name in the Hebrew tongue is* ***Abaddon****, but in the Greek tongue hath his name* ***Apollyon****.*
>
> ***12)*** *One woe is past; and, behold, there come two woes more hereafter.*

When God first woke me up to all that was happening in our day, He was explicit to me about this one. I was made to understand that this event is five months like flu season, that the enemy will take advantage of. The enemy will raise an army of Locust.

The Locust could not hurt those with the Seal of God, because they are already gone, caught up to Heaven.

Let me explain. This fallen star will cause Satan and the worst of hell to be released. Then the seventh head on the beast will suddenly appear. Satan will then know he has a short time and will implement his agenda quickly. Apollyon means the Destroyer.

Locusts are creatures that come in hordes, to devour, and do not leave any area untouched. They stay side by side and cover the ground systemically, and it is effective. This army works as locusts, but are really men and woman, of the military. They are not as natural Locusts that go after the grass, they only hurt men. So they are not really locust animals, but this is figurative. They have crowns as gold, which means they are given authority, following the ruling head, and carrying out orders, for the Destroyer.

Their job is to sting men with poison, as a scorpion does, for five months, or during flu season. This could be swine flu shots, with animal DNA, or any Ebola, or preventative shot of some sort. But it will be forced on us, because of the ramped diseases. I promise you they are not out to help you, but destroy your immune system, and corrupt your DNA. Do not trust them, and do not take this shot. They have micronanite technology these days that can stay in your system, and allow them to track you forever. This will make you very sick.

This event will wake you all up to how developed, trained, and strong your enemy has become while you were not looking. This is being planned right now, because they know the day is coming. The whole atmosphere will have changed. This is what God told me. They are waiting for the polar destruction, in order to have more control of the nations, and less people to deal with.

AN ARMY OF LOCUSTS

As a Thief in the Night

> Blow the trumpet in Zion; sound the alarm on my holy hill. Let all who live in the land tremble, for the day of the Lord is coming. It is close at hand—. A day of darkness and gloom, a day of clouds and blackness. Like dawn spreading across the mountains a large and mighty army comes, such as never was of old nor ever will be in ages to come. Before them fire devours, behind them a flame blazes. Before them the land is like the garden of Eden, behind them, a desert waste—nothing escapes them. They have the appearance of horses; they gallop along like cavalry. With a noise like that of chariots they leap over the mountaintops, like a crackling fire consuming stubble, like a mighty army drawn up for battle. At the sight of them, nations are in anguish; every face turns pale. They charge like warriors; they scale walls like soldiers. They all march in line, not swerving from their course. They do not jostle each other; <u>each marches straight ahead</u>. They plunge through defenses <u>without breaking ranks</u>. They rush upon the city; they run along the wall. <u>They climb into the houses</u>; like thieves they enter through the windows. Before them the <u>earth shakes</u>, the sky trembles, <u>the sun and moon are darkened</u>, and the stars no longer shine. The Lord thunders at the head of his army; his forces are beyond number, and mighty are those who obey his command. The <u>day of the Lord is great</u>; it is <u>dreadful.</u> Who can endure it? **(Joel 2:1–11)**

Rend Your Heart

"Even now," declares the Lord, "return to me with all your heart, with fasting and weeping and mourning." Rend your heart and not your garments. Return to the Lord your God, for he is gracious and compassionate, slow to anger and abounding in love, and he relents from sending calamity. Who knows? He may turn and have pity and leave behind a blessing—grain offerings and drink offerings for the Lord your God. Blow the trumpet in Zion, declare a holy fast, call a sacred assembly. Gather the people, consecrate the assembly; bring together the elders, gather the children, those nursing at the breast. Let the bridegroom leave his room and the bride her chamber. Let the priests, who minister before the Lord, weep between the temple porch and the altar. Let them say, "Spare your people, O Lord. Do not make your inheritance an object of scorn, a byword among the nations. Why should they say among the peoples, 'Where is their God?'" **(Joel 2:12–17)**

6. The Everlasting Gospel

REV 9:

13) *And the* ***sixth angel sounded****, and I heard a voice from the four horns of the golden altar which is before God,*

14) *Saying to the sixth angel which had the trumpet, Loose the four angels which are bound in the great river Euphrates.*

15) *And the four angels were loosed, which were prepared for an hour, and a day, and a month, and a year, for to slay the third part of men.*

16) *And the number of the army of the horsemen were two hundred thousand thousand: and I heard the number of them.* [That is 200,000,000]

17) *And thus I saw the horses in the vision, and them that sat on them, having breastplates of fire, and of jacinth, and brimstone: and the heads of the horses were as the heads of lions; and out of their mouths issued fire and smoke and brimstone.*

18) *By these three was the third part of men killed, by the fire, and by the smoke, and by the brimstone, which issued out of their mouths.*

> ***19)*** *For their power is in their mouth, and in their tails: for their tails were like unto serpents, and had heads, and with them they do hurt.*
>
> ***20)*** *And the rest of the men which were not killed by these plagues yet repented not of the works of their hands, that they should not worship devils, and idols of gold, and silver, and brass, and stone, and of wood: which neither can see, nor hear, nor walk:*
>
> ***21)*** *Neither repented they of their murders, nor of their sorceries, nor of their fornication, nor of their thefts.*

The Lord taught me what this passage meant twenty-five or so years ago, when I first became a soul winner. There are some real keys here to understand; this is where it helps, to fully understand what spiritual death to this world is.

Remember what I told you before, Jesus used the word dead when He was talking of the spiritual dead to this world (the Dead in Christ), like in Luke 9:60, Ephesians 5:14, and Colossians 2:20. *"Therefore if you be* ***dead*** *with* ***Christ*** *from the rudiments of the world, why, as though living in the world, are you subject to ordinances."* Also Romans 6:8.

The scripture here says there is just over thirteen months for an army of men and woman to kill (with the word and truth) a third of all people. They used fire and brimstone issuing out of their mouths. Fire and brimstone has only been used when referring to God's people. They had Breast-plates of Fire. That is only for God's people. The power to kill was in their mouths. This is spiritual death to the world, by an individual.

Here is the real KEY: In verse 20, it says, "and the rest of the men which were **not killed** by these plagues yet repented not of the works of their evil deeds." So that goes to say in essence, if the rest that did not die, yet did not repent, then the ones that died, did repent. Or all who died were those who repented to God, and dedicated their Lives to Jesus. This is a spiritual death to this world. This reality is of great significance.

So these Christians who were left behind, surviving the polar shift, had a short time to wake up as many as they could to what was really happening, and warning them, not to take the mark of the Beast, and repent to God, through Jesus Christ. They had to work quickly, because soon all the true believers would be in exile, to hide from the Beast, or Destroyers aggressive, deadly army. God's people will now be the enemy of the state, and the world.

Therefore, after the Rapture, there is the everlasting Gospel to preach, to all the Earth, those left behind. Tell everyone, "FEAR GOD, repent, receive Jesus as God's only Son, and refuse to worship, or take the mark of the Beast, unto your death." Remember in Revelation 9:15 the four angels came to help us get this gospel out. They don't have vials or wrath, these are good Angels, sent to help. They only had one year, one month, one day, and one hour. Well! That is very, very, very explicit. This is very important and is telling us we have a very short time to tell others, before LOCKDOWN. I feel this countdown starts from some notable event, like the polar reversal, in one hour. So if you survive this polar reversal note, that particular hour, and count one year, one month, one day, and an hour till you can't be free to preach anymore.

The day will come when no one can preach.

> "I must work the works of him that sent me, while it is day: the night cometh, when no man can work." **(John 9:4)**

If you find you are still here after the polar shift, try hard to keep track of the future days and months. Government may change our calendars even further. Count months by the moon, only twelve months is a year, not thirteen, as they have tried to add a month, every three years. And please don't forsake the assembly of yourselves with other believers.

THE GREAT REVIVAL

This may very well be the time of the last Great Revival the Christian World has been waiting for. A time when we will need to walk on water, heal the sick left and right, no deadly thing can harm us, food will multiply in our hands, and we will need to be supernaturally transported from one place to another in safety. Start to speak God's word boldly. This latter time should be the most supernatural time ever.

Revival message is below; as the MYSTERY of the seven thunders, are REVEALED.

> ***REV 10:***
>
> ***1)*** *And I saw another mighty angel come down from heaven, clothed with a cloud: and a rainbow was upon his head, and his face was as it were the sun, and his feet as pillars of fire:*
>
> ***2)*** *And he had in his hand a little book open: and he set his right foot upon the sea, and his left foot on the earth,*

3) *And cried with a loud voice, as when a lion roareth: and when he had cried, seven thunders uttered their voices.*

4) *And when the seven thunders had uttered their voices, I was about to write: and I heard a voice from heaven saying unto me, Seal up those things which the seven thunders uttered, and write them not.*

5) *And the angel which I saw stand upon the sea and upon the earth lifted up his hand to heaven,*

6) *And sware by him that liveth for ever and ever, who created heaven, and the things that therein are, and the earth, and the things that therein are, and the sea, and the things which are therein, that there should be time no longer:*

7) *But in the days of the voice of the seventh angel, when he shall begin to sound, the mystery of God should be finished, as he hath declared to his servants the prophets.*

8) *And the voice which I heard from heaven spake unto me again, and said, Go and take the little book which is open in the hand of the angel which standeth upon the sea and upon the earth.*

9) *And I went unto the angel, and said unto him, Give me the little book. And he said unto me, Take it, and eat it up; and it shall make thy belly bitter, but it shall be in thy mouth sweet as honey.*

10) *And I took the little book out of the angel's hand, and ate it up; and it was in my mouth sweet as honey: and as soon as I had eaten it, my belly was bitter.*

> ***11)*** *And he said unto me, Thou must prophesy again before many peoples, and nations, and tongues, and kings.*

The remaining must prophesy: In that short time left, they must let the people know that there is no more time, the Lord is coming soon, so be brave. It is a bittersweet pill. Many will instruct many in those days. So they had secret Bible studies and ate the book up.

Verse 7 speaks of deliverance just at the beginning sound of the seventh Trumpet, and there is time no longer. Time for all Christians stops, and all is now understood. This is saying only Gods remaining people will be reaped just before the Trumpet, which ushers in all Vials and Plagues.

And During this Time

> ***REV 11:***
>
> ***1)*** *And there was given me a reed like unto a rod: and the angel stood, saying, Rise, and measure the temple of God, and the altar, and them that worship therein.*
>
> ***2)*** *But the court which is without the temple leave out, and measure it not; for it is given unto the Gentiles: and the holy city shall they tread under foot forty and two months.*
>
> ***3)*** *And I will give power unto my two witnesses, and they shall prophesy a thousand two hundred and threescore days, clothed in sackcloth.*
>
> ***4)*** *These are the two olive trees, and the two candlesticks standing before the God of the earth.*

5) *And if any man will hurt them, fire proceedeth out of their mouth, and devoureth their enemies: and if any man will hurt them, he must in this manner be killed.*

6) *These have power to shut heaven, Athat it rain not in the days of their prophecy: and have power over waters to turn them to blood, and to smite the earth with all plagues, as often as they will.*

7) *And when they shall have finished their testimony, the beast that ascendeth out of the bottomless pit shall make war against them, and shall overcome them, and kill them.*

8) *And their dead bodies shall lie in the street of the great city, which spiritually is called Sodom and Egypt, where also our Lord was crucified.*

9) *And they of the people and kindreds and tongues and nations shall see their dead bodies three days and an half, and shall not suffer their dead bodies to be put in graves.*

10) *And they that dwell upon the earth shall rejoice over them, and make merry, and shall send gifts one to another; because these two prophets tormented them that dwelt on the earth.*

11) *And after three days and an half the Spirit of life from God entered into them, and they stood upon their feet; and great fear fell upon them which saw them.*

12) *And they heard a great voice from heaven saying unto them, Come up hither. And they ascended up to heaven in a cloud; and their enemies beheld them.*

13) *And the same hour was there a great earthquake, and the tenth part of the city fell, and in the earthquake were slain of men seven thousand: and the remnant were affrighted, and gave glory to the God of heaven.*

14) *The second woe is past; and, behold, the third woe cometh quickly.*

15) *And the* ***seventh angel sounded****; and there were great voices in heaven, saying, The kingdoms of this world are become the kingdoms of our Lord, and of his Christ; and he shall reign for ever and ever.* **[Jubilee Transfer]**

16) *And the four and twenty elders, which sat before God on their seats, fell upon their faces, and worshipped God,*

17) *Saying, We give thee thanks, O Lord God Almighty, which art, and wast, and art to come; because thou hast taken to thee thy great power, and hast reigned.*

18) *And the nations were angry, and thy wrath is come, and the time of the dead, that they should be judged, and that thou shouldest give reward unto thy servants the prophets, and to the saints, and them that fear thy name, small and great; and shouldest destroy them which destroy the earth.* **[Overcoming Christians are now caught up to Heaven.]**

19) *And the temple of God was opened in heaven, and there was seen in his temple the ark of his testament: and there were lightnings, and voices, and thunderings, and an earthquake, and great hail.*

Israel is taken over. Israel has its own problems. For three and a half years, there is a temple being built, and the enemy is controlling Israel. There are only a few secret places where the true worshipers meet. All areas are taken over.

The two Witnesses are probably Elijah and Enoch, the only two men known that never had to naturally die before the rapture. They have achieved the ability to completely die to Christ. But their prior experience was before Christ came. Now these two men will be used by God, to prophesy openly night and day. They are shaking up the enemy's camp, and Satan's people can't seem to control them. For these three and a half years, God's two men have miraculous power, and that foils a lot of the Beast's agenda.

Finally the Beast is able to kill and stop these two men, but they want to make an open example of them to all, and leave them laying there for all to see.

Now here is another key: These two men are left dead for three days right where Jesus was killed. Where Jesus was crucified is twenty feet above where the real ARK of the Covenant of God hidden in 586 BC, many years before Jesus's death. When Jesus was pierced by the soldier, there was an earthquake, and his blood spilled down the crack onto the left side of the mercy seat there underground below, fulfilling all the prophecies, and the Covenant.

This discovery was uncovered by Ron Wyatt, around 1980, and the authorities in Israel know about it now, but have been hiding this truth till they can win the wars, and build their temple. You can find the evidence at **www.arkdiscovery.com**.

So when God raises the two witnesses from the dead, and calls them to come up to heaven, there is again a great earthquake. Seven thousand die, and much of the ground collapsed at that spot. Verse 19 says that the Temple in Heaven was open and the Heavenly Ark could be seen. This would be the best time for God to present the Earthly Ark hidden there also, with the Ten Commandments, and show us all his glorious plan, and perfect finished work. How Jesus was the true Messiah, to all, and his testimony fulfills all, forever.

Verse 15 says all the kingdoms now belong to God, and this is probably where He will gather all his remaining elect to heaven. All Mysteries will now be revealed.

7. WOMAN SEEN IN THE SKY GIVES BIRTH

So now God wants to retell the story in a special way so we can know the timing, and the spiritual translation.

I had a recent dream. I was very pregnant, and God was saying the body of Christ is now full term.

God reiterates the story

REV 12:

1) *And there appeared a great wonder in heaven; a woman clothed with the sun, and the moon under her feet, and upon her head a crown of twelve stars:*

2) *And she being with child cried, travailing in birth, and pained to be delivered.*

3) *And there appeared another wonder in heaven; and behold a great red dragon, having seven heads and ten horns, and seven crowns upon his heads.*

4) *And his tail drew the third part of the stars of heaven, and did cast them to the earth: and the*

> *dragon stood before the woman which was ready to be delivered, for to devour her child as soon as it was born.*
>
> ***5)*** *And she brought forth a man child, who was to rule all nations with a rod of iron: and her child was caught up unto God, and to his throne.*

Virgo, Latin for virgin, the sign of the woman usually appears in late summer, in our sky, depending where on Earth you may live. The sun at her head and the moon at her feet lately has been September. There is Leo with nine stars at her head or above her. In September 23, 2017, Leo will be seen with three other planets, Mercury, Mars, and Venus. While this speculation of the possibility of fulfilling the twelve stars at the virgin's head sounds good, I have a more powerful theory.

Let us consider the new scientific discoveries found, Ceres, and 2003 UB313, updated by late 2013, since they have been diligently searching for the whereabouts of Planet X. They have found two other dwarf planets orbiting our sun. So with Nibiru, or Planet X, that adds up to twelve stars in our solar system. Since the scriptures mention the Sun and moon, as a reference point, and then twelve stars, that to me sounds like God is referencing our new found solar system, only surprisingly, revealed in this end time. God knew we would find them for such a time as this, and we would know, time is short. So look up. If this theory is true then Christ can come at any year when Virgo is, in the sky.

Various places see two suns now,
Nibiru, or Planet X.

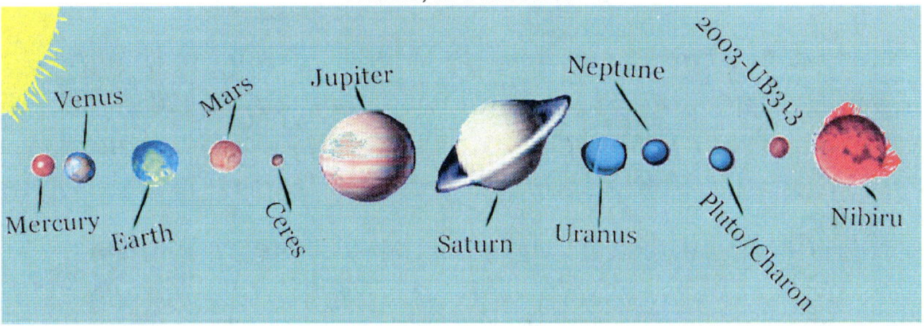

See our New Solar System

The woman, or the body of Christ, finally gives birth to a son, or Jesus, which is also the Dead in Christ. All the Earth has been convulsing and travailing for this day, the manifestation of the sons of God (Romans 8:19). The Rapture is the only real sign to all, that time is over, and the countdown is imminent.

In my vision, the Holy Spirit woke me to tell me the Red Dragon in the sky was this Red Planet X, coming in our solar system to create havoc. The Red Dragon represents Satan himself, whose kingdom is with the first beast, but he is actually the second beast. The first Beast is like John the Baptist, who was a forerunner for Jesus, but the first Beast is making a way for Satan. And then the rest of the fallen angels in the center of Earth, who have been locked up a while are loosed.

So the Man child, or the Bride EXITS, and Satan ENTERS the EARTH.

REV 12:

6) *And the woman fled into the wilderness, where she hath a place prepared of God, that they should feed her there a thousand two hundred and threescore days.*

7) *And there was war in heaven: Michael and his angels fought against the dragon; and the dragon fought and his angels,*

8) *And prevailed not; neither was their place found any more in heaven.*

9) *And the great dragon was cast out, that old serpent, called the Devil, and Satan, which deceiveth the whole world: he was cast out into the earth, and his angels were cast out with him.*

10) *And I heard a loud voice saying in heaven, Now is come salvation, and strength, and the kingdom of our God, and the power of his Christ: for the accuser of our brethren is cast down, which accused them before our God day and night.*

11) *And they overcame him by the blood of the Lamb, and by the word of their testimony; and they loved not their lives unto the death.*

12) *Therefore rejoice, ye heavens, and ye that dwell in them. Woe to the inhabiters of the earth and of the sea! for the devil is come down unto you, having great wrath, because he knoweth that he hath but a short time.*

13) *And when the dragon saw that he was cast unto the earth, he persecuted the woman which brought forth the man child.*

> ***14)*** *And to the woman were given two wings of a great eagle, that she might fly into the wilderness, into her place, where she is nourished for a time, and times, and half a time, from the face of the serpent.*
>
> ***15)*** *And the serpent cast out of his mouth water as a flood after the woman, that he might cause her to be carried away of the flood.*
>
> ***16)*** *And the earth helped the woman, and the earth opened her mouth, and swallowed up the flood which the dragon cast out of his mouth.*
>
> ***17)*** *And the dragon was wroth with the woman, and went to make war with the remnant of her seed, which keep the commandments of God, and have the testimony of Jesus Christ.*

The male Child is Christ, in us the hope of Glory. As the Bride is considered one flesh with Jesus, her Husband, the Child represents, the Bride, in Gods eyes, as one with Christ.

After this sign of the Child being caught up into heaven, the woman that gave birth, must flee for her life, away from the Dragon, who is chasing her. There are many bunkers that are set up to feed her for a forty-two-month period. The woman is the remaining Christians, who have survived this part of the tribulation, and are now waking up to understand. A lot of the attacks on the woman seem to be referring to a geographical area (flood after the woman, and the dragon goes after the remnant of her seed), so I feel the woman is the USA. More missionaries and evangelists have come out of her. The US has been for many years in protection of the Jews. Well, till now anyway!

Verse 11 is so important. We overcome by our words, standing for the truth and the blood of Christ. We must not give in to receive the mark of the Beast, or bow to him. We must not love our lives, even to the death. Most of those left will be tested.

The Dragon is cast out of heaven, and knows he has a short time to build his kingdom before God will stop him. His first agenda will be to try and drown those in the USA, with a great tsunami. This could be at the time of the polar reversal, or another incident. But I feel this is on the heels of the Rapture, and is at the same incident as the polar shift. The US will probably catch the worst of this reversal. Remember the enemy, knows this event is coming and could make it worst, blaming God. Just saying.

Then he will go after the rest of Christianity in the world and Jews. This is when they set up the NEW WORLD ORDER, killing all who do not comply.

PROPEHCY: Edgar Cayce told of this future Polar Shift event. In the early 1900s.

Edgar Cayce

8. BEAST FROM THE SEA

One World Order

REV 13:

1) *And I stood upon the sand of the sea, and saw a beast rise up out of the sea, having seven heads and ten horns, and upon his horns ten crowns, and upon his heads the name of blasphemy.*

2) *And the beast which I saw was like unto a leopard, and his feet were as the feet of a bear, and his mouth as the mouth of a lion: and the dragon gave him his power, and his seat, and great authority.*

3) *And I saw one of his heads as it were wounded to death; and his deadly wound was healed: and all the world wondered after the beast.*

The beast rising out of the sea is like a continent or entity rising out of many waters, or out of the people. This power had spots like a leopard, which is like many entities coming together, a swift united front. Its most muscle power is from Russia, and the Soviet Union. Its voice is as the USA and UK.

The first Beast has a leader, that has a real wound that looks as if, this wound was very deadly, like someone hacked his head with a sword. People think, "How could he still be alive?" and wonder after the Beast. Chapter 4 says that the dragon gave him his power, to prosper all over the world, blaspheme God, and come after God's people. He was possessed by Satan's right hand fallen angel, till Satan comes and takes his own seat, as the second Beast, pretending to be Christ.

Remember it is as if he were wounded, so the Beast with the wound does not have to actually die and be resurrected, as some teach.

REV 13:

4) *And they worshipped the dragon which gave power unto the beast: and they worshipped the beast, saying, Who is like unto the beast? who is able to make war with him?*

5) *And there was given unto him a mouth speaking great things and blasphemies; and power was given unto him* ***to continue*** *forty and two months.*

6) *And he opened his mouth in blasphemy against God, to blaspheme his name, and his tabernacle, and them that dwell in heaven.*

7) *And it was given unto him to make war with the saints, and to overcome them: and power was given him over all kindreds, and tongues, and nations.*

8) *And all that dwell upon the earth shall worship him, whose names are not written in the book of life of the Lamb slain from the foundation of the world.*

9) *If any man have an ear, let him hear.*

> ***10)*** *He that leadeth into captivity shall go into captivity: he that killeth with the sword must be killed with the sword. Here is the patience and the faith of the saints.*
>
> ***11)*** *And I beheld another beast coming up out of the earth; and he had two horns like a lamb, and he spake as a dragon.*

Verse 11, "Coming out of the Earth," is as someone coming out of a certain country, or entity. But it could also mean he comes from hell. He is pretending to be Christ, but speaks very rough and blasphemes everything Godly, and how religion is run.

The first Beast already has been reining, and he must have been coming to an end of his rein, because when this great disturbance comes he is given forty-two months to continue reigning.

I found out that our US president just got a bill passed and signed in 2013, that in a country catastrophe, he would be allowed to continue on and handle it. There would be no more elections. HUM! Suspicious! They know something.

> ***REV 13:***
>
> *12) And he exerciseth all the power of the first beast before him, and causeth the earth and them which dwell therein to worship the first beast, whose deadly wound was healed.*
>
> *13) And he doeth great wonders, so that he maketh fire come down from heaven on the earth in the sight of men,*

> ***14)*** *And deceiveth them that dwell on the earth by the means of those miracles which he had power to do in the sight of the beast; saying to them that dwell on the earth, that they should make an image to the beast, which had the wound by a sword, and did live.*
>
> ***15)*** *And he had power to give life unto the image of the beast, that the image of the beast should both speak, and cause that as many as would not worship the image of the beast should be killed.*

We will finally know what the **Name** of the beast is, or (New World Order), and what the 666 means, only when these ten religious leaders, called ten horns with crowns, are given their platform of prestige. The ten will make up the One World Religion.

They will make an image of the beast to worship. This image will be everywhere. On TV, or money, etc., sort of like my example below. Having commercials to promote it. The name will be catchy, and cause the number 666, like three *Vov*, the Hebrew letter for W, but looks like a 6.

World Wide Worship = 666

Remember the ten religious leaders are the ones in the public sight, but there may be many religions represented, by them, even Luciferian, or Atheistic.

The <u>second Beast</u> will cause us all, somehow to worship all at the same time when told, like in Daniels day, when the instruments played. Maybe during this commercial, we will be allowed to stop everything and worship. They do that 3 times a day now in Nazareth, Israel, with a loud speaker. Those who do not comply, or rebel, will become an instant negative example for all to see, and they will be killed. The Beasts wilding power, and new super technology, will amaze all, and terrify them.

REV 13:

16*) And he causeth all, both small and great, rich and poor, free and bond, to receive a <u>mark in their right hand</u>, or in their foreheads:*

> ***17)*** *And that no man might buy or sell, save he that had the mark, or the name of the beast, or the number of his name.*
>
> ***18)*** *Here is wisdom. Let him that hath understanding count the number of the beast: for it is the number of a man; and his number is Six hundred threescore and six.*

The Mark of the Beast is a number of a man, and every man on the earth has a number, like the Social Security number. On the chip they want to implant in us, will be the 666 first, to kick off the computer, followed by our personal number.

This is what an RFID chip might look like. They are implanting people now, in the meat between your right thumb and forefinger. Many coming over the borders, some sick, and in prison have been chipped. All who are designated for the FEMA camps will be chipped. The military are soon to be chipped.

Walmart chains all over the world now, have scanners for the right hand and forehead. So far a thief can easily hack your information from these chips by passing by you with a scanner device. **Taking the Chip is not a good idea, any way you look at it.** The chip will be tracking, all our bank information, medical records, SSN, etc. And has some kind of a liquid we don't know about. Any thief can scan and tap into your whole purchasing personality and preferences.

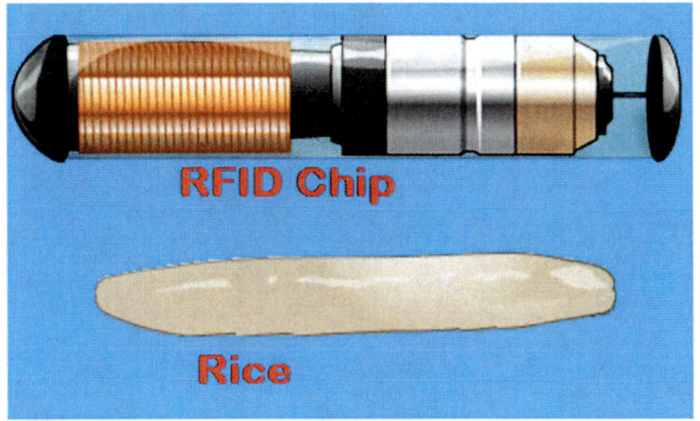

Obama Care RFID Microchip implant simulation.

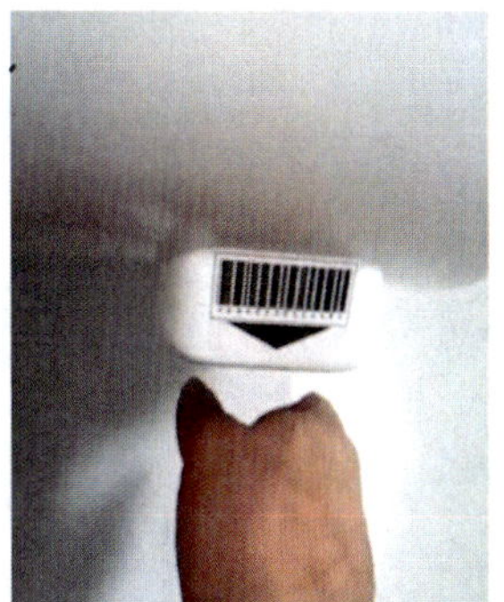

Walmart scanners.

This chip is a drawing, but in the real chip there has been found a liquid. No one knows what it is for, and it is not show here. Is it poison they can stop or kill you with instantly? Is it a DNA changer to start controlling us? It has been proven that if you are hit with a burst of microwave, this chip will explode. A sudden solar flare could do this, and we are then all very sick.

> *And the first went, and poured out his vial upon the earth; and there fell a* ***noisome and grievous sore*** *upon the men which had the mark of the beast, and upon them which worshipped his image.* **(Rev 16:2) [POP & BURN]**

> *And the smoke of their torment ascendeth up for ever and ever: and they have no rest day nor night, who worship the beast and his image, and whosoever receiveth the mark of his name.* **(Rev 14:11)**

And the beast was taken, and with him the false prophet that wrought miracles before him, with which he deceived ***them that had received the mark*** *of the beast, and them that worshipped his image. These both* ***were cast alive into a lake of fire burning with brimstone.*** **(Rev 19:20)**

9. GOD'S RECAP CHAPTER

REV 14:

1*) And I looked, and, lo, a Lamb stood on the mount Zion, and with him a hundred forty and four thousand, having his Father's name written in their foreheads.*

2*) And I heard a voice from heaven, as the voice of many waters, and as the voice of a great thunder: and I heard the voice of harpers harping with their harps:*

3*) And they sung as it were a new song before the throne, and before the four beasts, and the elders: and no man could learn that song but the hundred and forty and four thousand, which were redeemed from the earth.*

4*) These are they which were not defiled with women; for they are virgins. These are they which follow the Lamb whithersoever he goeth. These were redeemed from among men, being the first-fruits unto God and to the Lamb.*

5*) And in their mouth was found no guile: for they are without fault before the throne of God.*

These are the Raptured, Jesus' own Bride.

Meaning: BLAMELESS, SPOTLESS, WITHOUT GUILE, OF A FIRST FRUIT, OF A VIRGIN STATE.

Obviously, in order to be the Bride of Christ, a person must be saved, have given their whole life to Christ, and Spirit filled because "those who are led by the Spirit are the children of God."

Please see my chapter at the back, on "GOD'S CHAMPIONS." It will explain what these 144,000 had going for them, that qualified them to be Raptured, and escape the Tribulation.

> ***REV 14:***
>
> ***6)*** *And I saw another angel fly in the midst of heaven, having the* ***<u>everlasting gospel to preach</u>*** *unto them that dwell on the earth, and to every nation, and kindred, and tongue, and people,*
>
> *7) Saying with a loud voice,* ***<u>Fear God,</u>*** *and give glory to him; for the hour of his judgment is come: and worship him that made heaven, and earth, and the sea, and the fountains of waters.*
>
> ***8)*** *And there followed another angel, saying, Babylon is fallen, is fallen, that great city, because she made all nations drink of the wine of the wrath of her fornication.*

After the Rapture, devastation, trials with the Beast, this is the last chance everlasting Gospel to preach, to all the Earth, those left behind. Tell everyone again, "FEAR GOD, repent, receive Jesus as God's only son, and refuse to worship or take the mark of the Beast unto your death." Remember in Revelation 9:15, the four angels came to help us, and two witnesses came to get this gospel out. They only had one year, one month, one day, and one hour. Well! We are down to the wire, in the last minutes.

Our reward is coming, OUR INCENTIVE below.

> *He that leadeth into captivity shall go into captivity: he that killeth with the sword must be killed with the sword. Here is the patience and the faith of the saints.* **(Rev 13:10)**
>
> *Here is the patience of the saints: here are they that keep the commandments of God, and the faith of Jesus. And I heard a voice from heaven saying unto me, Write,* ***Blessed*** *are the dead which die in the Lord from henceforth: Yea, saith the Spirit, that they may rest from their labours; and their works do follow them.* **(Rev 14:12–13)**

Again, the day will come when no one can preach. John 9:4 says, "I must work the works of him that sent me, while it is day: the night cometh, when no man can work." Also, blessed are those who spiritually die to this world, and also physically die, in the Lord.

Also, this is where the two witnesses will come in. THANK GOD.

> ***REV 14:***
>
> ***9)*** *And the third angel followed them, saying with a loud voice, If any man worship the beast and his image, and receive his mark in his forehead, or in his hand,*

> ***10)*** *The same shall drink of the wine of the wrath of God, which is poured out without mixture into the cup of his indignation; and he shall be tormented with fire and brimstone in the presence of the holy angels, and in the presence of the Lamb:*
>
> ***11)*** *And the smoke of their torment ascendeth up for ever and ever: and they have no rest day nor night, who worship the beast and his image, and whosoever receiveth the mark of his name.*
>
> ***12)*** *Here is the patience of the saints: here are they that keep the commandments of God, and the faith of Jesus.*
>
> ***13)*** *And I heard a voice from heaven saying unto me, Write, Blessed are the dead which die in the Lord from henceforth: Yea, saith the Spirit, that they may rest from their labours; and their works do follow them.*

There is a crown for those who overcome. Here is the patience and hope of the saints, also what befalls the ones who take the Mark of the Beast.

Here Is More Proof of the Rapture and Second Coming

> ***REV 14:***
>
> ***14)*** *And I looked, and behold a white cloud, and upon the cloud one sat like unto the Son of man, having on his head a golden crown, and in his hand a sharp sickle.*
>
> ***15)*** *And another angel came out of the temple, crying with a loud voice to him that sat on the*

> *cloud,* ***Thrust in thy sickle****, and reap: for the time is come for thee to reap; for the harvest of the earth is ripe.*
>
> ***16)*** *And he that sat on the cloud thrust in his sickle on the earth; and the earth was reaped.*

KEY: FIRST the BRIDE RAPTURE, and Sickle reaping by and with Jesus on a cloud, as seen before.

> ***REV 14:***
>
> ***17)*** *And another angel came out of the temple which is in heaven, he also having a sharp sickle.*
>
> ***18)*** *And another angel came out from the altar, which had power over fire; and cried with a loud cry to him that had the sharp sickle, saying, Thrust in thy sharp sickle, and gather the clusters of the vine of the earth; for her grapes are fully ripe.*
>
> ***19)*** *And the angel* ***thrust in his sickle*** *into the earth, and gathered the vine of the earth, and cast it into the great winepress of the wrath of God.*
>
> ***20)*** *And the winepress was trodden without the city, and blood came out of the winepress, even unto the horse bridles, by the space of a thousand and six hundred furlongs.*

KEY: SECOND COMING of this Sickle reaping by an Angel who has power over FIRE. Both the Rapture and Second Coming, are just prior to a different great disaster. The disaster is on their heels.

I had a terrible car accident in the year 2000, in which I experienced the feeling of being taken prior to an incident. I was driving, and the car and I went into a super SLOW MOTION, which was witnessed by a bystander. I was snatched out a foot from my body before the impact, and watched it all from out of my body. I remember thinking, what happened? I saw my arms and head get all cut up. Then after the car stopped, I was put back in my body, when I felt the pain. I had broken bones, but I really never was there when it happened. So will it be in the end. If we are found true to God and the Gospel of Christ, we will be spared.

10. SEVEN LAST PLAGUES

REV 15:

1*) And I saw another sign in heaven, great and marvellous, seven angels having the <u>seven last plagues</u>; for in them is filled up the wrath of God.*

2*) And I saw as it were a sea of glass mingled with fire: and them that had gotten the victory over the beast, and over his image, and over his mark, and over the number of his name, stand on the sea of glass, having the harps of God.*

3*) And they sing the song of Moses the servant of God, and the song of the Lamb, saying, Great and marvellous are thy works, Lord God Almighty; just and true are thy ways, thou King of saints.*

4*) Who shall not fear thee, O Lord, and glorify thy name? for thou only art holy: for all nations shall come and worship before thee; for thy judgments are made manifest.*

5*) And after that I looked, and, behold, the temple of the tabernacle of the testimony in heaven was opened:*

6) And the seven angels came out of the temple, having the seven plagues, clothed in pure and white linen, and having their breasts girded with golden girdles.

7) And one of the four beasts gave unto the seven angels seven golden vials full of the wrath of God, who liveth for ever and ever.

***8)** And the temple was filled with smoke from the glory of God, and from his power; and no man was able to enter into the temple, till the seven plagues of the seven angels were fulfilled.*

Seven last plagues are only for those left behind, who took the mark of the Beast, and worshiped the beast, and of course for the Beast and his minions.

Those who got the victory are taken up, and all eyes will see it. Heaven is opened, and the Ark is seen, the testimony in heaven.

Note: In verse 8, none of these left who worshiped the Beast will be able to enter the heavenly temple till all is fulfilled. They will not be able to escape. They will seek death and will not find it.

The Seven Vials are as the plagues of Egypt.

REV 16:

1) And I heard a great voice out of the temple saying to the seven angels, Go your ways, and pour out the vials of the wrath of God upon the earth.

***2**) And the **first** went, and poured out his vial upon the earth; and there fell a noisome and grievous sore upon the men which had the mark of the beast, and upon them which worshipped his image.*

***3**) And the **second angel** poured out his vial upon the sea; and it became as the blood of a dead man: and every living soul died in the sea.*

***4)** And the **third angel** poured out his vial upon the rivers and fountains of waters; and they became blood.*

***5**) And I heard the angel of the waters say, Thou art righteous, O Lord, which art, and wast, and shalt be, because thou hast judged thus.*

***6**) For they have shed the blood of saints and prophets, and thou hast given them blood to drink; for they are worthy.*

7) And I heard another out of the altar say, Even so, Lord God Almighty, true and righteous are thy judgments.

***8**) And the **fourth angel** poured out his vial upon the sun; and power was given unto him to scorch men with fire.*

***9**) And men were scorched with great heat, and blasphemed the name of God, which hath power over these plagues: and they repented not to give him glory.*

***10**) And the **fifth angel** poured out his vial upon the seat of the beast; and his kingdom was full of darkness; and they gnawed their tongues for pain,*

11) *And blasphemed the God of heaven because of their pains and their sores, and repented not of their deeds.*

12) *And the* ***sixth angel*** *poured out his vial upon the great river Euphrates; and the water thereof was dried up, that the way of the kings of the east might be prepared.*

13) *And I saw three unclean spirits like frogs come out of the mouth of the dragon, and out of the mouth of the beast, and out of the mouth of the false prophet.*

14) *For they are the spirits of devils, working miracles, which go forth unto the kings of the earth and of the whole world, to gather them to the battle of that great day of God Almighty.*

15) *Behold,* ***I come as a thief.*** *Blessed is he that watcheth, and keepeth his garments, lest he walk naked, and they see his shame.*

16) *And he gathered them together into a place called in the Hebrew tongue Armageddon.*

17) *And the seventh angel poured out his vial into the air; and there came a great voice out of the temple of heaven, from the throne, saying****, It is done****.*

18) *And there were voices, and thunders, and lightning's; and there was a great earthquake, such as was not since men were upon the earth, so mighty an earthquake, and so great.*

19) *And the great city was divided into three parts, and the cities of the nations fell: and great Babylon came in remembrance before God, to give unto her the cup of the wine of the fierceness of his wrath.*

> ***20)*** *And every island fled away, and the mountains were not found.*
>
> ***21)*** *And there fell upon men a great hail out of heaven, every stone about the weight of a talent: and men blasphemed God because of the plague of the hail; for the plague thereof was exceeding great.*

Jesus comes as a Thief. Only those watching for Christ will escape.

In verse 17, "It is done." The final plague is the FINALE. Now Armageddon, and there was a great quake as none before, felt all over Earth. This is not the quake from the polar shift, it is another.

NUKE TIME: I really feel this is referring to a great bomb, the big one is here. It splits the USA in three. The mountains are flattened, and Islands literally are moved, and a great hail, of fallout all over the world.

I say this is America that splits in three, with confidence, because I had a prophetic friend named Dawn who is now in heaven. She once told me around 1998 that she had a vision and literally saw America split in three sections. She had been right about so many things, that I tucked her information away for when I would need to know that.

11. THIS IS THE JUDGMENT OF THE GREAT WHORE

REV 17:

1) *And there came one of the seven angels which had the seven vials, and talked with me, saying unto me, Come hither; I will show unto thee the judgment of the great whore that sitteth upon many waters:*

2) *With whom the kings of the earth have committed fornication, and the inhabitants of the earth have been made drunk with the wine of her fornication.*

3) *So he carried me away in the spirit into the wilderness: and I saw a woman sit upon a scarlet coloured beast, full of names of blasphemy, having seven heads and ten horns.*

4) *And the woman was arrayed in purple and scarlet colour, and decked with gold and precious stones and pearls, having a golden cup in her hand full of abominations and filthiness of her fornication:*

5) *And upon her forehead was a name written, MYSTERY, BABYLON THE GREAT, THE*

MOTHER OF HARLOTS AND ABOMINATIONS OF THE EARTH.

Purple or scarlet refers to having sin, which both she and the beast have. They probably broke all ten commandments, but mostly this has to do with God himself, or religion (ongoing masquerading as god, spirit of control, manipulation, deception, death, stealing for lavish living). She has peace and riches, what no one else has, and causes all to marvel, and sell out to her, in order to get some of what she has, but never can obtain. She is Great Babylon, the evil Spirit behind the agenda, the alluring seduction, and deception. This spirit reigned in Babylon of old, and moved to different continents, but is seemingly now here in the USA.

(At Revelation 17:18, the same figurative woman is described as "the great city that has a kingdom over the kings of the earth." The term "city" indicates an organized group of people. Since this "great city" has control over "the kings of the earth," the woman named Babyloan the Great must be an influential organization that is international in scope. It can rightly be called a world empire. What kind of empire? A religious one. Like the Pope in Rome, but everywhere in the world too. Notice how some related passages in the book of Revelation lead us to this conclusion.) This now looks like the US. By the way God is not religious.

REV 17:

6) *And I saw the woman drunken with the blood of the saints, and with the blood of the martyrs of Jesus: and when I saw her, I wondered with great admiration.*

7) And the angel said unto me, Wherefore didst thou marvel? I will tell thee the mystery of the woman, and of the beast that carrieth her, which hath the seven heads and ten horns.

***8)** The beast that thou sawest was, and is not; and shall ascend out of the bottomless pit, and go into perdition: and they that dwell on the earth shall wonder, whose names were not written in the book of life from the foundation of the world, when they behold the beast that was, and is not, and yet is.*

THE BEAST is SATAN'S SEAT. Satan himself was working here, on Earth before the flood, and was locked up till now, and is NOW LOOSED for A SEASON. Till now we were only dealing with Satan's kingships, and minions beneath him. When he comes, things will be horrid. But God must make His point, of what life without God would be, because most of us are not getting the point yet, of why we should choose Christ. Remember it was so bad back in Noah's day that God had to literally destroy all of mankind with the flood, except the eight. Also, we have seen Hitler's work, and that was not Satan himself yet. We need to wake up. This satanic coming will be a taste of Hell.

REV 17:

***9)** And here is the mind which hath wisdom. The seven heads are seven mountains, on which the woman sitteth.*

***10)** And there are seven kings: five are fallen, and one is, and the other is not yet come; and when he cometh, he must continue a short space.*

Mountains are indicative of known civilizations of land. The Beast controls all SEVEN CONTINENTS, or the world.

In the end there will be seven kings, notable to us on the whole earth (five of their kingdoms were each powerful at one time, but not dominant anymore. One is powerful now, probably the US, and the only short timer one is Satan's kingdom. The one which will dominate over all, then. Probably Russia, China, the UK, Israel, Rome, US, then Satan's kingdom with his minions like ISIS influence.)

> ***REV 17:***
>
> ***11)*** *And the beast that was, and is not, even he is the eighth, and is of the seven, and goeth into perdition.*

Satan's Seat is of one predominate Country head. HE IS EVIL, and a power entity HIMSELF, as the eighth head, but is also of one of these seven heads possessing in a man, as a king. Two in one, and could be rising in the US. Just saying.

> ***REV 17:***
>
> ***12)*** *And the ten horns which thou sawest are ten kings, which have received no kingdom as yet; but receive power as kings one hour with the beast.*
>
> ***13)*** *These have one mind, and shall give their power and strength unto the beast.*

Ten top religions will form, like false Christianity, Islam, Hinduism, Buddhism, Atheists, Judaism, Shintoism, Catholic, New Age, or Satanism. These ten don't have real kings yet but they will in the end. They (multitudes of people as waters, the Whore sits on) will join together as a force, and unknowingly give Satan his power. Also they hate the whore, and plot to destroy her, probably will destroy the US. There are many prophesy's against the US out there.

REV 17:

14) *These shall make war with the Lamb, and the Lamb shall overcome them: for he is Lord of lords, and King of kings: and they that are with him are called, and chosen, and faithful.*

15) *And he saith unto me, The waters which thou sawest, where the whore sitteth, are peoples, and multitudes, and nations, and tongues.*

16) *And the ten horns which thou sawest upon the beast, these shall hate the whore, and shall make her desolate and naked, and shall eat her flesh, and burn her with fire.*

17) *For God hath put in their hearts to fulfil his will, and to agree, and give their kingdom unto the beast, until the words of God shall be fulfilled.*

18) *And the woman which thou sawest is that great city, which reigneth over the kings of the earth.*

THE US: Here is one prophesy.

Excerpt of AA Allen's 1954 Vision of the United States being Attacked by Nukes

(...)Then suddenly I saw from the Atlantic and from the Pacific, and out of the Gulf, rocket-like objects that seemed to come up like fish leaping out of the water. High into the air they leaped, each headed in a different direction, but every one towards the U.S. On the ground, the sirens screamed louder. And up from the ground I saw similar rockets begin to ascend. To me, these appeared to be interceptor rockets although they arose from different points all over the U.S. However, none of them seemed to be successful in intercepting the rockets that had risen from the ocean on every side. These rockets finally reached their maximum height, slowly turned over, and fell back toward the earth in defeat. Then suddenly, the rockets which had leaped out of the ocean like fish all exploded at once. The explosion was ear-splitting. The next thing which I saw was a huge ball of fire. The only thing I have ever seen which resembled the thing I saw in my vision was the picture of the explosion of the H-bomb in the South Pacific. In my vision, it was so real I seemed to fall, as a searing heat came from it. As the vision spread before my eyes, and I viewed the widespread desolation brought about by the terrific explosions,

I could not help thinking, "While the defenders of our nation have quibbled over what means of defense to use, and neglected the only true means of defense, faith and dependence upon the true and living God, the thing which she greatly feared has come unto her! How true it has proven that Unless the LORD guards the city, The watchman keeps awake in vain (Psalm 127).

Then as the noise of the battle subsided, to my ears came this quotation from Joel, the second chapter, Blow ye the trumpet in Zion, and sound an alarm in my holy mountain:

let all the inhabitants of the land tremble: for the day of the LORD cometh, for it is nigh at hand; A day of darkness and of gloominess, a day of clouds and of thick darkness, as the morning spread upon the mountains: a great people and a strong; there hath not been ever the like, neither shall be any more after it, even to the years of many generations.

- END AA ALLEN'S VISION -

BOMBS SHOOTING FROM OUT OF THE WATER, we have this technology today, just saying.

In One Hour Babylon Is Fallen

REV 18:

1) *And after these things I saw another angel come down from heaven, having great power; and the earth was* ***lightened with his glory*****.** **[NUKE – FLASH]**

2) And he cried mightily with a strong voice, saying, Babylon the great is fallen, is fallen, and is become the habitation of devils, and the hold of every foul spirit, and a cage of every unclean and hateful bird.

3) For all nations have drunk of the wine of the wrath of her fornication, and the kings of the earth have committed fornication with her, and the merchants of the earth are waxed rich through the abundance of her delicacies.

4) And I heard another voice from heaven, saying, Come out of her, my people, that ye be not partakers of her sins, and that ye receive not of her plagues. **[PLAGUES with an 'S.]**

This shows that God has made provision to take His people home before all plagues. This places the Second Coming at the Seventh Trump, and Christians delivered before all plagues.

REV 18:

5) For her sins have reached unto heaven, and God hath remembered her iniquities.

6) Reward her even as she rewarded you, and double unto her double according to her works: in the cup which she hath filled fill to her double.

There may be two bombs.

REV 18:

7) How much she hath glorified herself, and lived deliciously, so much torment and sorrow give her:

for she saith in her heart, I sit a queen, and am no widow, and shall see no sorrow.

8) *Therefore shall her plagues come in one day, death, and mourning, and famine; and she shall be utterly burned with fire: for strong is the Lord God who judgeth her.*

9) *And the kings of the earth, who have committed fornication and lived deliciously with her, shall bewail her, and lament for her, when they shall see the smoke of her burning,*

10) *Standing afar off for the fear of her torment, saying, Alas, alas, that great city Babylon, that mighty city! for in one hour is thy judgment come.*

11) *And the merchants of the earth shall weep and mourn over her; for no man buyeth their merchandise any more:*

12) *The merchandise of gold, and silver, and precious stones, and of pearls, and fine linen, and purple, and silk, and scarlet, and all thyine wood, and all manner vessels of ivory, and all manner vessels of most precious wood, and of brass, and iron, and marble,*

13) *And cinnamon, and odours, and ointments, and frankincense, and wine, and oil, and fine flour, and wheat, and beasts, and sheep, and horses, and chariots, and slaves, and souls of men.*

14) *And the fruits that thy soul lusted after are departed from thee, and all things which were dainty and goodly are departed from thee, and thou shalt find them no more at all.*

***15**) The merchants of these things, which were made rich by her, shall stand afar off for the fear of her torment, weeping and wailing,*

***16**) And saying, Alas, alas, that great city, that was clothed in fine linen, and purple, and scarlet, and decked with gold, and precious stones, and pearls!*

***17**) For in one hour so great riches is come to nought. And every shipmaster, and all the company in ships, and sailors, and as many as trade by sea, stood afar off,*

***18)** And cried when they saw the smoke of her burning, saying, What city is like unto this great city!*

***19**) And they cast dust on their heads, and cried, weeping and wailing, saying, Alas, alas, that great city, wherein were made rich all that had ships in the sea by reason of her costliness! for in one hour is she made desolate.*

***20**) Rejoice over her, thou heaven, and ye holy apostles and prophets; for God hath avenged you on her.*

***21**) And a mighty angel took up a stone like a great millstone, and cast it into the sea, saying, Thus with violence shall that great city Babylon be thrown down, and shall be found no more at all.*

***22**) And the voice of harpers, and musicians, and of pipers, and trumpeters, shall be heard no more at all in thee; and no craftsman, of whatsoever craft he be, shall be found any more in thee; and the sound of a millstone shall be heard no more at all in thee;*

> ***23)*** *And the light of a candle shall shine no more at all in thee; and the voice of the bridegroom and of the bride shall be heard no more at all in thee: for thy merchants were the great men of the earth; for by thy sorceries were all nations deceived.*
>
> ***24)*** *And in her was found the blood of prophets, and of saints, and of all that were slain upon the earth.*

Again, all wealth of any kind has passed through her, and she has profited from it. This is the Greatest bombing ever seen, of all times, and will break up the USA in three parts. Judgment comes to this city but it is to take down all demonic forces that have killed all the saints, from the beginning. Devils last forever, and find new hosts, when their hosts die.

12. GIVE HONOR TO GOD FOR HE IS JUST, AND FOR THE MARRIAGE OF THE LAMB IS COME.

"The JUDGMENT"

REV 19:

1*) And after these things I heard a great voice of much people in heaven, saying, Alleluia; Salvation, and glory, and honour, and power, unto the Lord our God:*

2*) For true and righteous are his judgments: for he hath judged the great whore, which did corrupt the earth with her fornication, and hath avenged the blood of his servants at her hand.*

3*) And again they said, Alleluia. And her smoke rose up for ever and ever.*

4*) And the four and twenty elders and the four beasts fell down and worshipped God that sat on the throne, saying, Amen; Alleluia.*

5) *And a voice came out of the throne, saying, Praise our God, all ye his servants, and ye that fear him, both small and great.*

6) *And I heard as it were the voice of a great multitude, and as the voice of many waters, and as the voice of mighty thunderings, saying, Alleluia: for the Lord God omnipotent reigneth.*

7) Let us be glad and rejoice, and give honour to him: for the marriage of the Lamb is come, and his wife hath made herself ready.

8) *And to her was granted that she should be arrayed in fine linen, clean and white: for the fine linen is the righteousness of saints.*

9) *And he saith unto me, Write, Blessed are they which are called unto the marriage supper of the Lamb. And he saith unto me, These are the true sayings of God.*

10) *And I fell at his feet to worship him. And he said unto me, See thou do it not: I am thy fellowservant, and of thy brethren that have the testimony of Jesus: worship God: for the testimony of Jesus is the spirit of prophecy.*

11) *And I saw heaven opened, and behold a white horse; and he that sat upon him was called Faithful and True, and in righteousness he doth judge and make war.*

12) *His eyes were as a flame of fire, and on his head were many crowns; and he had a name written, that no man knew, but he himself.*

13) *And he was clothed with a vesture dipped in blood: and his name is called The Word of God.*

***14**) And the armies which were in heaven <u>followed him upon white horses</u>, clothed in fine linen, white and clean.*

***15**) And out of his mouth goeth a sharp sword, that with it he should smite the nations: and he shall rule them with a rod of iron: and he treadeth the winepress of the fierceness and wrath of Almighty God.*

***16**) And he hath on his vesture and on his thigh a name written, KING OF KINGS, AND* LORD *OF* LORD*S.*

***17**) And I saw an angel standing in the sun; and he cried with a loud voice, saying to all the fowls that fly in the midst of heaven, Come and gather yourselves together unto the supper of the great God;*

***18**) That ye may eat the flesh <u>of kings</u>, and the flesh of captains, and the flesh of <u>mighty men</u>, and the flesh of horses, and of them that sit on them, and the flesh of all men, both free and bond, both small and great.*

***19**) And I saw the beast, and the kings of the earth, and their armies, gathered together to make war against him that sat on the horse, and against his army.*

***20**) <u>And the beast was taken</u>, and with him the false prophet that wrought miracles before him, with which he deceived them that had received the mark of the beast, and them that worshipped his image. These both were cast alive <u>into a lake of fire</u> burning with brimstone.*

***21)** And the remnant were slain with the sword of him that sat upon the horse, which sword proceeded out of his mouth: and all the fowls were filled with their flesh.*

LAST WHITE HORSE BATTLE: To destroy all kings, mighty, rich, and all kingdoms on Earth, and they are all thrown in the lake of fire, who are not in the Book of Life.

Judgment of Heaven and Earth

REV 20:

***1)** And I saw an angel come down from heaven, having the key of the bottomless pit and a great chain in his hand.*

***2)** And he laid hold on the dragon, that old serpent, which is the Devil, and Satan, and bound him a thousand years,*

***3)** And cast him into the bottomless pit, and shut him up, and set a seal upon him, that he should deceive the nations no more, till the thousand years should be fulfilled: and after that he must be loosed a little season.*

***4)** And I saw thrones, and they sat upon them, and judgment was given unto them: and I saw the souls of them that were beheaded for the witness of Jesus, and for the word of God, and which had not worshipped the beast, neither his image, neither had received his mark upon their foreheads, or in their hands; and they lived and reigned with Christ a thousand years.*

5) But the rest of the dead lived not again until the thousand years were finished. This is the first resurrection.

6) Blessed and holy is he that hath part in the first resurrection: on such the second death hath no power, but they shall be priests of God and of Christ, and shall reign with him a thousand years.

7) And when the thousand years are expired, Satan shall be loosed out of his prison,

8) And shall go out to deceive the nations which are in the four quarters of the earth, Gog and Magog, to gather them together to battle: the number of whom is as the sand of the sea.

9) And they went up on the breadth of the earth, and compassed the camp of the saints about, and the beloved city: and fire came down from God out of heaven, and devoured them.

10) And the devil that deceived them was cast into the lake of fire and brimstone, where the beast and the false prophet are, and shall be tormented day and night for ever and ever.

11) And I saw a great white throne, and him that sat on it, from whose face the earth and the heaven fled away; and there was found no place for them.

12) And I saw the dead, small and great, stand before God; and the books were opened: and another book was opened, which is the book of life: and the dead were judged out of those things which were written in the books, according to their works.

13) And the sea gave up the dead which were in it; and death and hell delivered up the dead which

> *were in them: and they were judged every man according to their works.*
>
> ***14)*** *And death and hell were cast into the lake of fire. This is the second death.*
>
> ***15)*** *And whosoever was not found written in the book of life was cast into the lake of fire.*

A great Reward is given to all those who have overcome, and they get to rule and reign with the Lord a thousand years. The earth gave up her dead, that were overcomers, and this is the first resurrection. Blessed are those who can be a part of the first resurrection. They will be judged now, and allowed in heaven, and have no part of the second death.

But the rest of those who did not overcome, were not resurrected, but remained asleep, through that thousand years. Then Satan shall be loosed from his prison for a short time, to try and deceive many, to come to a final battle, testing those who had not had a chance to overcome yet. Maybe the new born generations during this one thousand years. The saints win the battle and the Earth is destroyed. Satan and the false prophet, and their cohorts were thrown in the Lake of Fire.

The book of life is open and all the people that were on earth were judged, and those who were not in the book were cast in the lake of fire also. This is the second death.

13. THE NEW HEAVEN AND THE NEW EARTH

REV 21:

1*) And I saw a new heaven and a new earth: for the first heaven and the first earth were passed away; and there was no more sea.*

2*) And I John saw the holy city, new Jerusalem, coming down from God out of heaven, prepared as a bride adorned for her husband.*

3*) And I heard a great voice out of heaven saying, Behold, the tabernacle of God is with men, and he will dwell with them, and they shall be his people, and God himself shall be with them, and be their God.*

4*) And God shall wipe away all tears from their eyes; and there shall be no more death, neither sorrow, nor crying, neither shall there be any more pain: for the former things are passed away.*

5*) And he that sat upon the throne said, Behold, I make all things new. And he said unto me, Write: for these words are true and faithful.*

> ***6)*** *And he said unto me, It is done. I am Alpha and Omega, the beginning and the end. I will give unto him that is athirst of the fountain of the water of life freely.*
>
> *7) He that overcometh shall inherit all things; and I will be his God, and he shall be my son.*
>
> ***8)*** *But the fearful, and unbelieving, and the abominable, and murderers, and whoremongers, and sorcerers, and idolaters, and all liars, shall have their part in the lake which burneth with fire and brimstone: which is the second death.*

All evildoers and liars are thrown in the lake of Fire. But those that overcome are now called the sons and daughters of God.

The New Jerusalem comes as a Bride, bright, shiny, new. The essence of God is in men now, God dwells in us, and all rivers are life, and only come from the throne of God. God is true and faithful to make all things new.

> ***REV 21:***
>
> ***9)*** *And there came unto me one of the seven angels which had the seven vials full of the seven last plagues, and talked with me, saying, Come hither, I will show thee the bride, the Lamb's wife.*
>
> ***10)*** *And he carried me away in the spirit to a great and high mountain, and showed me that great city, the holy Jerusalem, descending out of heaven from God,*
>
> ***11)*** *Having the glory of God: and her light was like unto a stone most precious, even like a jasper stone, clear as crystal;*

12) *And had a wall great and high, and had twelve gates, and at the gates twelve angels, and names written thereon, which are the names of the twelve tribes of the children of Israel:*

13) *On the east three gates; on the north three gates; on the south three gates; and on the west three gates.*

14) *And the wall of the city had twelve foundations, and in them the names of the twelve apostles of the Lamb.*

15) *And he that talked with me had a golden reed to measure the city, and the gates thereof, and the wall thereof.*

16) *And the city lieth foursquare, and the length is as large as the breadth: and he measured the city with the reed, twelve thousand furlongs. The length and the breadth and the height of it are equal.*

17) *And he measured the wall thereof, an hundred and forty and four cubits, according to the measure of a man, that is, of the angel.*

18) *And the building of the wall of it was of jasper: and the city was pure gold, like unto clear glass.*

19) *And the foundations of the wall of the city were garnished with all manner of precious stones. The first foundation was jasper; the second, sapphire; the third, a chalcedony; the fourth, an emerald;*

20) *The fifth, sardonyx; the sixth, sardius; the seventh, chrysolite; the eighth, beryl; the ninth, a topaz; the tenth, a chrysoprasus; the eleventh, a jacinth; the twelfth, an amethyst.*

21) *And the twelve gates were twelve pearls; every several gate was of one pearl: and the street of the city was pure gold, as it were transparent glass.*

22) *And I saw no temple therein: for the Lord God Almighty and the Lamb are the temple of it.*

23) *And the city had no need of the sun, neither of the moon, to shine in it: for the glory of God did lighten it, and the Lamb is the light thereof.*

24) *And the nations of them which are saved shall walk in the light of it: and the kings of the earth do bring their glory and honour into it.*

25) *And the gates of it shall not be shut at all by day: for there shall be no night there.*

26) *And they shall bring the glory and honour of the nations into it.*

27) *And there shall in no wise enter into it any thing that defileth, neither whatsoever worketh abomination, or maketh a lie: but they which are written in the Lamb's book of life.*

If the bride is New Jerusalem, then land is important to God, and why He fights for Jerusalem on earth. God wants to live in His people.

God and Jesus is the light of this city, and the temple of it. Saying God wants us to live in Him also. There is no more evil in this city, and the doors are never shut.

"We shall live in the house of the lord forever."

REV 22:

***1)** And he showed me a pure river of water of life, clear as crystal, proceeding out of the throne of God and of the Lamb.*

***2)** In the midst of the street of it, and on either side of the river, was there the tree of life, which bare twelve manner of fruits, and yielded her fruit every month: and the leaves of the tree were for the healing of the nations.*

***3)** And there shall be no more curse: but the throne of God and of the Lamb shall be in it; and his servants shall serve him:*

***4)** And they shall see his face; and his name shall be in their foreheads.*

***5)** And there shall be no night there; and they need no candle, neither light of the sun; for the Lord God giveth them light: and they shall reign for ever and ever.*

***6)** And he said unto me, These sayings are faithful and true: and the Lord God of the holy prophets sent his angel to show unto his servants the things which must shortly be done.*

7) Behold, I come quickly: blessed is he that keepeth the sayings of the prophecy of this book.

***8)** And I John saw these things, and heard them. And when I had heard and seen, I fell down to worship before the feet of the angel which showed me these things.*

***9)** Then saith he unto me, See thou do it not: for I am thy fellowservant, and of thy brethren the prophets, and of them which keep the sayings of this book: worship God.*

10) *And he saith unto me, Seal not the sayings of the prophecy of this book: for the time is at hand.*

11) He that is unjust, let him be unjust still: and he which is filthy, let him be filthy still: and he that is righteous, let him be righteous still: and he that is holy, let him be holy still.

12) *And, behold, I come quickly; and my reward is with me, to give every man according as his work shall be.*

13) *I am Alpha and Omega, the beginning and the end, the first and the last.*

14) *Blessed are they that do his commandments, that they may have right to the tree of life, and may enter in through the gates into the city.*

15) *For without are dogs, and sorcerers, and whoremongers, and murderers, and idolaters, and whosoever loveth and maketh a lie.*

16) *I Jesus have sent mine angel to testify unto you these things in the churches. I am the root and the offspring of David, and the bright and morning star.*

17) *And the Spirit and the Bride say, Come. And let him that heareth say, Come. And let him that is athirst come. And whosoever will, let him take the water of life freely.*

18) *For I testify unto every man that heareth the words of the prophecy of this book, If any man shall add unto these things, God shall add unto him the plagues that are written in this book:*

19) *And if any man shall take away from the words of the book of this prophecy, God shall take away* *his part out of the book of life, and out of the holy city, and from the things which are written in this book.*

20) *He which testifieth these things saith, Surely I come quickly. Amen. Even so, come, Lord Jesus.*

21) *The grace of our Lord Jesus Christ be with you all. Amen.*

It is very plane in verse 11 that how we are when we die in the end is how we will stay, forever. We cannot change anymore. That is very sobering, and we need to prepare ourselves for this eternity. We can only change here on Earth, this is a great opportunity. Angels can't do what we can do. Not all will be able to See God, or enter the city, so take care not to miss out.

The Bride will tell others, saying come to Jesus. All who call on Jesus will be saved, but only at this time on Earth, it is too late after death. Jesus will come for his Bride, those who love his appearing.

WARNING: After Christ's true Rapture, and the polar shift, Satan may try and fake a rapture and say he is Christ on Earth. If anyone tells you Christ is here or there on Earth, that is fake. Christ is coming to get us and battle evil from the sky. He will never again come to live as a human on Earth, so please do not be fooled by a false Christ.

14. THE BOOK OF THE PROPHET DANIEL

And My Vision

In one of my early morning visions, I saw this polar reversal as leading to the desolation, in the book of Daniel. Then I heard the Holy Spirit say, that this coming polar destruction, and the coming *One World Religion* agenda uniting the gods, leads to the Abomination 0f Desolation spoken of in Daniel.

So I got up and took all day to study the book of Daniel, and hear the Holy Spirit speak. The Holy Spirit showed me that in the end, True Christians would be protected as Daniel was with the Lions, and the 3 Hebrew men were in the fire. But on the reverse side many, like the majority will be deceived, to think uniting Religions is peace and a very good idea.

It would be nicer to think that all we have to do is watch from afar, one evil man just sit in a newly built temple, in another small land, Israel, that gets attacked and think, this is the Abomination of desolation in Daniel. While we sit protected in our own safe lands. But it is not that simple. The abomination of desolation is going to be worldwide. No one will have to tell you of it, you will be directly involved, and know it yourself. Sorry to say.

The Holy Spirit told me, when the prophets in the Bible were talking of God's Temple being defiled by Satan in the end, they were not referring to a building, but God's people, as His Temple. When Satan will finally force all people to take the mark of the Beast, it will *truly* be an Abomination. Eventually in the end, the Jews are determined to rebuild a building that is as God's temple in the past, regardless many times God's Temple buildings have been defiled. Even now there is a mosque built there. Defiling a building is not what is meant here, but God in us, His holy Temples.

Satan is trying to take God's place in us all, with the mark of the Beast. If we refuse, Satan will have us destroyed, in the end, which is desolation. Even if a person takes the mark, it is an everlasting desolation to him, separation from God forever, no return. This Abomination will make Desolation, and the two are the same huge event.

In Daniel 12:11, the word <u>sacrifice</u> was not in the original text. It should be saying, "And from the time that the daily <u>routine</u> shall be taken away, and the abomination that maketh desolate set up, there shall be a thousand two hundred and ninety days." The daily routine will definitely be disrupted after, three days of darkness and the polar reversal, nothing will ever be the same, for all people.

Young's literal translation of Hebrew, says in Daniel 12:11, "...And from the time of the turning aside of the <u>perpetual</u>, and to the giving out of the <u>desolating abomination</u>, are days a thousand, two hundred, and ninety." Many are having visions, and dreams, of the mark of the beast, or a forced agenda upon Christians. But I have never heard anyone dream of an Antichrist sitting in a rebuilt temple. When Jesus died the curtain separating the Holy of Holies from the people was torn in half from the top to the bottom, which says we are to be his holy place now. God no longer dwells in a building, but He now dwells in men, woman, and children.

So likewise in Matthew 24:15: "When ye therefore shall see the *abomination of desolation*, spoken of by Daniel the prophet, *stand in the holy place*, (whoso readeth, let him understand)," they are referring to this event. We must then understand that standing in the Holy Place is standing for the one true God, Jesus, and His Righteousness, not taking the mark of the Beast.

Desolating Abomination: When considering the timing of Jesus coming, Daniel 12:11–12 tells us about the Abomination being set up in 1,290 days, and then the desolation, saying, "But blessed are those who wait till the 1,335th day." There is a forty-five-day difference here, and this could be our only warning time.

This could be a time from the polar shift disruption, having the One World Government set up to only be able to buy and sell with the chip imbedded in your hand, for 1,290 days. Then forty-five day of forcing all who resisted to take the mark or be killed, at the very end, to the 1,335th day, from the polar shift.

Themes in the Book of Daniel include heroism, remaining true to God in the midst of an adverse and idolatrous culture, and God's protection of his faithful ones through his Angels. Chapters 1 to 6 refer to the trials of Daniel and his three young companions, Hananiah, Mishael, and Azariah, during the time of the great Kings of the East. Their names, all of which reflect the name of God, are changed to names referring to Babylonian idols. Shadrach, Meshach, and Abednego are saved from the fiery furnace by an angel in Chapter 3. Chapter 6 describes Daniel in the Lions' Den, where an angel saved Daniel by shutting the mouths of the lions. Chapters 7 to 12 reveal the angels Gabriel and Michael in the apocalyptic visions. Daniel 12:2 is one of the rare passages in the Old Testament that refers to the Resurrection of the Dead.

The Book of Daniel serves as the only apocalyptic book of the Old Testament, as Chapters 7 to 12 foretell the End Times. The great nations of the world have risen against the Lord, but God will protect His people and His Kingdom shall prevail and last forever. Jesus in calling himself, the Son of Man in Daniel 7:13, and is also referenced in Revelation 14:14.

Now let's compare two Visions in Daniels book.

In Daniel 10:2-7

In those days I Daniel was mourning three full weeks. I ate no pleasant bread, neither came flesh nor wine in my mouth, neither did I anoint myself at all, till three whole weeks were fulfilled. And in the four and twentieth day of the first month, as I was by the side of the great river, which is Hiddekel, or Tigris; Then I lifted up mine eyes, and looked, and behold a certain man clothed in linen, whose loins were girded with fine gold of Uphaz: His body also was like the beryl, and his face as the appearance of lightning, and his eyes as lamps of fire, and his arms and his feet like in colour to polished brass, and the voice of his words like the voice of a multitude. And I Daniel alone saw the vision: for the men that were with me saw not the

> *vision; but a great quaking fell upon them, so that they fled to hide themselves.*

RAPTURE: Daniel's vision is of Jesus, the brightness of His being, coming in the clouds, during an earthquake. The voice of multitudes shows many people joining with him.

A clue here is that this vision happened to him on the first month, the 25th day, of the Jewish calendar. That is from March to April to us, around Passover.

Note: Daniel was seeking, and saw the Lord, and was not in the quake, but those with him, did not see, and were busy in a quake. The others hid themselves in the rocks, as in the reference of Revelation 6.

Daniel is suggesting that if you are not seeking Jesus, you will not see Him coming. And you will be left in the quake.

> In **Daniel 12:1–4:** And at that time shall Michael stand up, the great prince which standeth for the children of thy people: and there shall be a time of trouble, such as never was since there was a nation even to that same time: and at that time thy people shall be delivered, every one that shall be found written in the book. And many of them that sleep in the dust of the earth shall awake, some to everlasting life, and some to shame and everlasting contempt. And they that be wise shall shine as the brightness of the firmament; and they that turn many to righteousness as the stars for ever and ever. But thou, O Daniel, shut up the words, and seal the book, even to the time of the end: many shall run to and fro, and knowledge shall be increased.

> And in **Daniel 12:9:** And he said, Go thy way, Daniel: for the words are closed up and sealed till the time of the end.

SECOND COMING: This is a second reference of a catching up. But this one does not reference any quake, just terrible trouble. It seems to be referring to the very end of it all.

This may very well b referencing two separate events coming. First the seeking Bride, then those left behind to fight to the end, refusing the mark of the beast. As in Revelation 12, where there was a woman that gave birth to a son, which the dragon wanted to devour. However the babe was caught up in heaven, first. Then the woman was tormented and fled for three and a half years.

Also there are two separate, reaping events mentioned in Revelation 14:15–19. One from the son of man, mentioned in the cloud, and the second of an Angel with power over fire. This second reaping says the grapes are fully ripe, and goes on to mention the wine press and blood to the horses bridle. Sounds like the very end.

> For the Lord himself shall descend from heaven with a shout, with the voice of the archangel, and with the trump of God: and the dead in Christ shall rise first: **Then we** which are alive and remain shall be caught up together with them in the clouds, to meet the Lord in the air: and so shall we ever be with the Lord. Wherefore comfort one another with these words. **(1 Thes 4:16–18)**

The dead in Christ is referring to the Spiritual dead to this world, Bride of Christ, which has risen first. The left behind in Christ now need comfort. This verse here is speaking *solely* to those left behind, saying, "Then we which remain," depicting those in Christ which remained after the polar shift. This is telling of two different incidents. The dead in Christ rising first, and those which had remained behind are now rising (I call the Second Coming, so not to get confused). To God time is irrelevant. To Him forty-two months between the two incidents is a blink. A thousand years is as a day.

> And through his policy also he shall cause craft to prosper in his hand; and he shall magnify himself in his heart, and by peace shall destroy many: he shall also stand up against the Prince of princes; but he shall be broken without hand. **(Dan 8:25)**

The Holy Spirit told me the name Grecia, in Daniel Chapter 8, is America. America is the only country I know that has really caused craft to prosper. Babylon with King Nebuchadnezzar is trying to come back alive today.

> Then Nebuchadnezzar the king sent to gather together the princes, the governors, and the captains, the judges, the *treasurers*, the counsellers, the sheriffs, and all the rulers of the provinces, to come to the dedication of the image which Nebuchadnezzar the king had set up. Then the princes, the governors, and captains, the judges, the treasurers, the counsellers, the sheriffs, and all the rulers of the provinces, were gathered together unto the dedication of the image that Nebuchadnezzar the king had set up; and they stood before the image that Nebuchadnezzar had set up. Then

> an herald cried aloud, To you it is commanded, O people, *nations*, and languages, That at what time ye hear the sound of the *cornet, flute, harp, sackbut, psaltery, dulcimer, and all kinds of music*, ye fall down and worship the golden image that Nebuchadnezzar the king hath set up: And whoso falleth not down and worshippeth shall the same hour be cast into the midst of a burning fiery furnace. **(Dan 3:2–6)**

This shows the New World Order will control the musical media, singers, rock stars, and the like as some are today, expecting us all to worship by idolizing them, and how they are controlled by Satan, even giving the hand sign of the two horns, and symbolic subliminal. The number 11 is also widely used.

Also you see how the king gathers all the people in high places to the dedication, showing how all the rich, famous, people in high places today are also being corrupted.

Also Daniel refused the king's meat in chapter 8, just as we should refuse some of the poisons the media is giving us today. And a lot of the symbolism in Daniel is now being used in this One World Agenda today. The Beast portrayed in chapter 7 is the same as in the book of Revelation.

15. "GOD'S CHAMPIONS"

Like in that song, "All He Wanted Was My Heart," I feel there is much truth here. Really, all God wants is our heart. He doesn't have it if we have given it to the enemy in any way. You must be born again, giving your life to Christ, first. See a prayer at the end of this book.

In studying those godly men that made it big, in that they knew how to get Miracles from God, AA Allan and such, I learnt that in every situation, these people had an encounter with God that instructed them how to live a life, separated from the world. Mostly this happened after a time of an extensive fast. Knowing this secret, and doing your best to reach it, is very important if you want to do anything big for God.

Before I was called by the Lord to be a soul winner, I had a spiritual encounter, which would drive me to just want to consume the scriptures on Christ and all about soul winning. I couldn't get enough. My household chores suffered a bit in those days. But this is how God reached me.

During that time, I came to a scripture that really popped out at me. It said, "You must be blameless, spotless, without guile, of a first fruit, and of a virgin state." It hit me in my heart that this is a key. I reread this over and over trying to memorize it.

I even wrote these five points down. In the weeks to come, I repeated this scripture over and over.

I went on to become a heavy Soul winner. The Lord used me in a mighty way, with persecution. I have a CD series about my soul wining teaching, available to purchase that can be found at the end of this book.

But the kicker was that after ten years I wanted to put this five-point verse in a teaching, and I could not find it. I looked and looked, but found it did not exist. The verse was only put there supernaturally for me to find. The five points are true, and can be found in the scriptures individually, but this scripture I have been saying for years, that sums up so perfectly, what a person needs to do to really please the Father, cannot be found.

BLAMELESS, SPOTLESS, WITHOUT GUILE, A FIRST FRUIT, OF A VIRGIN STATE.

None of this works without the gift of the Holy Spirit, so pray and ask for this Gift. No man need teach you but the Holy Spirit.

> But if from thence thou shalt seek the Lord thy God, thou shalt find him, if thou seek him with all thy heart and with all thy soul. **(Deut 4:29)**

Here are the meanings of the five points God gave me.

BLAMELESS

Not blaming others, and fulfilling the Commandments, faultless.

> Judge not, that ye be not judged. For with what judgment ye judge, ye shall be judged: and with what measure ye mete, it shall be measured to you again. And why beholdest thou the mote that is in thy brother's eye, but considerest not the beam that is in thine own eye? **(Matt 7:1–3)**
>
> And they were both righteous before God, walking in all the commandments and ordinances of the Lord blameless. (**Luke 1:6**)
>
> Who shall also confirm you unto the end, that ye may be blameless in the day of our Lord Jesus Christ. (**1 Cor 1:8**)
>
> That ye may be blameless and harmless, the sons of God, without rebuke, in the midst of a crooked and perverse nation, among whom ye shine as lights in the world. (**Phil 2:15**)
>
> And the very God of peace sanctify you wholly; and I pray God your whole spirit and soul and body be preserved blameless unto the coming of our Lord Jesus Christ. (**1 Thes 5:23**)

Here is where you must learn to forgive. It is easier than you think. I had to learn that even forgiveness is a gift of God. We as humans are not really capable of overcoming these things. Try as we may we will always fall back. So here is how I learned to overcome and forgive.

When the Holy Spirit, or the enemy brings up what happened to you, just say, "I forgive this person in the name of Jesus, and I forgive myself. I plead the precious blood of Jesus over the sins here, and the Light of God over the Soul Wounds." As time goes on the Holy Spirit will bring up deeper hidden things, as you pray over every one. Eventually there will be only a clear heart, and the wounds will be healed, supernaturally. This method works.

Yes, you will be tested in the future, but now you know how to handle it, so it never takes a root again. You will become an overcomer that can hear God.

SPOTLESS

Keep praying, "I am the righteousness of God through the blood of Jesus."

The Blood of Jesus makes us clean, without spot. You must ask forgiveness, and receive Jesus as Lord, and what he did for you on the cross.

> For then shalt thou lift up thy face without spot; yea, thou shalt be stedfast, and shalt not fear. **(Job 11:15)**
>
> What Jesus did, that he might present it to himself a glorious church, not having spot, or wrinkle, or any such thing; but that it should be holy and without blemish. (**Eph 5:27**)
>
> That thou keep this commandment without spot, unrebukable, until the appearing of our Lord Jesus Christ. (**1 Tim 6:14**)
>
> How much more shall the blood of Christ, who through the eternal Spirit offered himself without spot to God, purge your conscience from dead works to serve the living God? (**Heb 9:14**)
>
> But with the precious blood of Christ, as of a lamb without blemish and without spot. (**1 Pet 1:19**)

WITHOUT GUILE

A lie is anything that exalts itself against the knowledge of God and his word.

This is not just talking about cuss words, but speaking faith, in love. Scripture says "Let the poor say I am rich.", and the sick are healed, by the blood of Jesus. Your experience may say you are poor, or sick, but the truth is you are rich and the healed of the Lord. If you speak the lie (what we see) then that is what you get. You give power to it. It is said in 2 Corinthians 5:7, "We walk by faith and not by sight."

Heaven

And there shall in no wise enter into it any thing that defileth, neither whatsoever worketh abomination, or maketh a lie: but they which are written in the Lamb's book of life. (**Rev 21:27**)

And in their mouth was found no guile: for they are without fault before the throne of God. (**Rev 14:5**)

Ephesians 4: [Read all of this chapter]

1) I therefore, the prisoner of the Lord, Beseech you that ye walk worthy of the vocation wherewith ye are called,

5) One Lord, one faith, one baptism, One God.

15) But speaking the truth in love, may grow up into him in all things, which is the head, even Christ:

> **25)** Wherefore putting away lying, speak every man truth with his neighbour: for we are members one of another.
>
> **29)** Let no corrupt communication proceed out of your mouth, but that which is good to the use of edifying, that it may minister grace unto the hearers. And grieve not the holy Spirit of God, whereby ye are sealed unto the day of redemption.

FIRST FRUITS

The Holy Spirit told me this comes only with the washing of the water of the WORD. Read the Bible, and pray. It changes your DNA.

> This I say therefore, and testify in the Lord, that ye henceforth walk not as other Gentiles walk, in the vanity of their mind, **(Eph 4:17)**
>
> And be renewed in the spirit of your mind; And that ye put on the new man, which after God is created in righteousness and true holiness. (**Eph 4:23–24**)
>
> The husbandman that laboureth must be first partaker of the fruits. (**2 Tim 2:6**)
>
> But the wisdom that is from above is first pure, then peaceable, gentle, and easy to be intreated, full of mercy and good fruits, without partiality, and without hypocrisy. (**James 3:17**)

Jesus is the Word and came to bring us back to God. Sin is separation from God. Repenting is turning away from evil toward God. The truth of the word draws us away from sin, because if you have sin the love of the father is not in you, the two can't stand together. Perfect love casts out all fear, it takes fear captive. Fear is all variations of condemnation. If you have fear you are not made perfect in love. Jesus, the word is the way, the truth, and the life back to God.

The BRIDE is FIRST FRUITS: The Dead in Christ shall *rise first*, and *then we* which remain shall be caught up together with Him in the sky. Bride is the first catching ups.

Interestingly, in the old days the Priest would burn one sacrifice, and let the second sacrifice go free, I feel that is like the two catching ups. One is caught up free and Holy, and the other bears the iniquity, and is burnt, then Holy. Yes, I do know Jesus was the pure sacrifice. I am just stating my noticed analogies, so they may possibly help you, understand things better.

VIRGIN STATE

This is *not* talking of being a solitary single virgin. What the lord is saying here is that we are not to be defiled with the Whore's system in Revelation, woman sitting on the Beast. Most of the gods named in the Old Testament were all goddesses. The term here refers to other gods. The first, second, and third commandments.

So be as a Virgin having only one God, come back to your first and only love Jesus. You can love Him in the person of the Father, Son Jesus, or Holy Spirit. The trinity only is God. God said that if you do not have the Son, you do not have the Father.

Prophets are not gods. Leaders are not gods. Statues are not gods. Saints are not gods. We can never be god. Mary is not god. Satan is not god. Angels are not gods, and they will tell you do not bow to them. Be not controlled with bad habits, people, or things, which consume or control you. For example, Alcohol can be a god to you, if you can't walk away. On the door of liquor stores they even tell you, you're buying Spirits here. Now is the time for sacrifices.

This is not to say that any type of perverted or free sex, is ever allowed. Anything that has a hook on you takes you away from God. Like the Word says; "come out from among her", that is from the world's way. Ask forgiveness, and turn from it.

Revelation 14:1-4

1) *And I looked, and, lo, a Lamb stood on the mount Zion, and with him a hundred forty and four thousand, having his Father's name written in their foreheads.* [FOCUSED ON HIM ONLY.]

2) *And I heard a voice from heaven, as the voice of many waters, and as the voice of a great thunder: and I heard the voice of harpers harping with their harps:*

3) *And they sung as it were a new song before the throne, and before the four beasts, and the elders: and no man could learn that song but the hundred and forty and four thousand, which were redeemed from the earth.*

4) These are they which were not defiled with women; for they are virgins. These are they which follow the Lamb whithersoever he goeth. ***These were redeemed from among men, being the firstfruits unto God and to the Lamb.***

Do not take the mark of the Beast. Don't join the New World Order. Having many gods is definitely out. Take time to know

Jesus personally. This could also have to do with our DNA. See the next chapter.

> ***Matthew 25:* The 10 Virgins please read the entire chapter**
>
> ***1)*** *Then shall the kingdom of heaven be likened unto ten virgins, which took their lamps, and went forth to meet the bridegroom.*
>
> ***10)*** *And while they went to buy, the bridegroom came; and they that were ready went in with him to the marriage: and the door was shut.*
>
> ***12)*** *But he answered and said, Verily I say unto you, I know you not.*
>
> ***13)*** *Watch therefore, for ye know neither the day nor the hour wherein the Son of man cometh.*

16. "OUR DNA"

The Words of Jesus Are Literal.

To His True Set-Apart Bride in these End Times. We need to be petitioning and repenting for our DNA and ask for the pure DNA of Christ to take over. Our DNA must be born again.

Science is revealing the truth in the Bible. Scientists have proved the God element in our DNA. The mystery of the "seed of the serpent" versus the "seed of the woman." **The DNA Structure—the Battle of Good and Evil.**

There is a confirmation in Daniel 2:43, the problem where "they" mingle themselves with the seed of man.

We are in a spiritual battle that manifests in the natural, and though the war is already won, if we would just start to apply the Blood of the Lamb, we would start to taste victory and freedom. Our weapon is the blood of the Lamb (which carries Yehoshua's DNA) because it is the fullness of I Am's love, poured out for our salvation, redemption, deliverance, healing, freedom, and the word of our testimony applying the blood.

Jesus's DNA was a single helix, and at the fall we somehow received another helix, so we now have two strands. This was proven by Ron Wyatt, when he discovered the actual Ark of the Covenant, with the Ten Commandments in a cave, twenty feet below where Jesus was crucified. The discovery was around 1980. Authorities in Israel know about it and are hiding the information till the best time. You can see this discovery at **www.arkdiscovery.com**. After the quake at the time of Jesus's death, the earth opened up and exposed enough to let the Blood from His pierced side drip onto the Ark buried below. It then closed again, sealing the Covenant in heaven and on Earth. God is awesome.

Ron was allowed by the Angel to have some blood tested and it was found that Jesus only had one helix in His DNA. Humans have 46 chromosomes in their genes, 23 from each parent. Christ had only 23 total plus a Y chromosome. See **www.arkdiscovery.com**.

The tree of knowledge of good and evil must have been tampered with by the enemy, so there was corrupt DNA present when Adam and Eve ate the fruit of it. So now all offspring have this double DNA. Receiving Christ's pure blood puts a deposit in us, which can start to reverse this process. Especially if we feed it enough.

Having a double nature means our DNA has two choices on every gene that it can choose. DNA always chooses the strongest gene. It is geared that way for survival. So if we feed the good gene we will eventually turn good, and if we feed it bad, we will eventually turn all bad. Evil is progressive. If we just don't try to feed it, our gene will turn bad, left to itself. But only by receiving that perfect deposit of the Blood of our

Savior, by Salvation, can we even hope to repair it. God said He is faithful to forgive if we ask, and that means He is bound by covenant, to give all who ask, that deposit and a chance. We can go as far as we want with it. There is, in the spirit, a very real deposit going on. The bible says Satan can't touch that deposit that is in you, but he can mess with your nature if you don't stop him by feeding the good.

NOW CONSIDER: If we allow the enemy to inject more DNA into us, by taking the mark, our DNA will start to form a third helix. It is like eating from the bad tree again. The bible says; in Matt 18:19 that if two or more agree it has to happen. So consider this example. Two boys are walking along, and one is very passive. The other says: let's go and take the air out of the tires, from that man's car, giggling. The other says sheepishly, ah-ok! The law is set and they will do it because they agreed. These boys will find themselves doing what they did not really want to do because of agreement.

So it is with our DNA. Jesus is in us to help agree with us to go back to the good side. But if we allow this third helix, this internal battle will be heavily slanted to go evil. Two against one. You decide. Please do not take the mark of the Beast.

Don't be fooled, the enemy wants to corrupt our DNA even further by adding a third helix that will insure our evil nature and control us. This process is then irreversible, because our natures will be too far gone. We must not take the Mark of the Beast, trust me. Even such as an allegiance with the enemy could start this irreversible, degenerating process.

The Bible says that as in the days of Noah, so shall it be in the end, there were giants, and they were DNA corrupt. There is no doubt that we are in a DNA battle with the enemy. This would explain the abductions. It would explain why God had to send a flood, and how it is that Adam and Eve were able to generate a sin nature on all of us. It would explain the need for blood sacrifice. Perhaps the tree of Good and Evil was DNA corrupt. We can't deny the battle within our own minds and body.

So I feel our DNA is important enough to mention, that we need to repent, and not allow the enemy to inject any more corruption.

When we receive Jesus, we receive his DNA deposit.

Back in Revelation 12, they overcame Satan by the blood of the Lamb and the word of their testimony. Your testimony is the Word of God you speak.

Jesus has given His DNA, or blood, for our DNA. Each one of His shed cells had someone's name on it.

There is no forgiveness of sin without the shedding of blood, Hebrews 9:22. That is when one's perfect DNA blood speaks up for another, how it is passed.

Back in the day animal sacrifice had to be pure without blemish. Adam and Eve sinned, but not the animals yet, though we humans and devils must have ruined their gene pool by now. Jesus set a voice of purpose for His sacrifice, he gave it for us all. That is how it becomes ours, but we must take it, and nurture it to grow, with our mouths, speaking the Word of God.

Hebrews 11:1: "Now faith is a substance of things hoped for, the evidence of things not seen." Faith is what we speak.

Faith is a substance, like putty or clay, it is tangible. Faith is a real tangible, a spiritual force. When Jets started to fly at

Mock speed, that is the speed of sound, they heard a loud sonic boom. After that the piolets reported they saw many waves of all frequencies and colors across the sky. It was very majestic, they were seeing sound. These words were going to the ends of Earth to carry their purpose. They were real, beautiful, and seemed powerful.

Sin is separation from God. Sin is not doing the evil things listed in the Ten Commandments. Doing evil is proof sin exists in you, or your DNA. Jesus in essence said, you committed it already, in your heart, not your mind. Like Hate is the start of Murder, and Lust is the start of Adultery, and when it is finally committed, it is only proof that sin existed in your DNA, or heart garden.

Faith is the substance manifested, that Hope is present. Murder is the substance proof that intense hate is present, caused by entertaining thoughts of evil.

John 1:19 indicates Jesus was the Word made flesh, God's Word. The heavens were framed by God's word. Our DNA is framed by His Word spoken.

Faith won't work in your mind, Faith works in your heart. God wants our heart. So, contrary to most belief, the battle is not in your mind, it is in your heart, which develops your DNA decisions, what gene we choose. We are drawn away by our own lust, what is in us.

Romans 8:7: "The carnal mind is enmity against God, and not subject to the laws of God; neither indeed can it be." So the change cannot take place here. This is why so many intelligent people have a hard time with faith, or even believing God is real. This is why Jesus said we must come as little children. Children bypass the mind, of reason.

Out of the abundance of the heart the mouth speaks. Seed grows in your heart and changes your DNA. You must circumcise your heart.

Romans 10:6 "Righteousness which is of Faith speaks on this wise, say not in thine heart…."

Romans 10:8 "The word is nigh you, even in your mouth, and your heart."

To be Righteous you must activate Jesus's Gene pool, which is the Word of God, as Jesus was the Word. Matthew 6:33: "Seek first the kingdom of God, (His Word), and His righteousness; and all these things will be added to you."

Hebrew 10:23 "Let us hold fast the profession of our faith without wavering; for He is faithful that promised it."

17. MY THEORIES

Finally, I must tell you my theories on timing.

The four blood moons are a sign to us, first to start looking up, and get us ready looking for these two feast days, of Passover and Sukkot. I believe with all my heart, that these two feast times will be used in the time of both the Rapture, and the Second Coming.

First Fruits usually is a spring happening into summer. Depending on location and type of Grapes, Grape season is harvested either February to April for the South, and August to October in the North. Pray that your Flight be not in the winter, or Sabbath. (The seventh Day of Rest, the next one thousand years), because it is a time of great trouble.

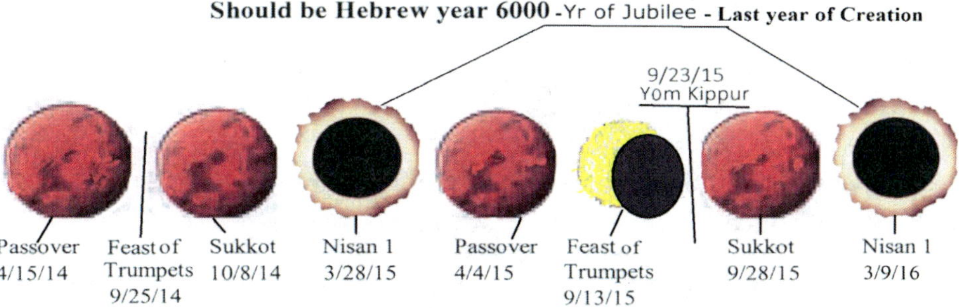

God sets our Calendar back to correct days.

I feel that because we perverted our calendar so bad, God had to give us a clue of the true days, and pointed them out, and set them again. You see here there are ten or eleven days difference between the holidays of one year to another. This would be correct. The following year, 2016, our calendar might be adding a month. That will not be correct. As this example above we must subtract ten or eleven days every year to stay correct. God bless your efforts to keep up.

Solar Eclipse on Nisan 1 is a sign of Judgment, and we have two. I feel this is our correct Jubilee Year.

The total solar eclipse on March 20 falls on Nisan 1, which is the first day of the first month of the biblical calendar. According to Jewish tradition, a solar eclipse on Nisan 1 is a sign of judgment. And this has certainly been true in the past. For example, there was a solar eclipse on Nisan 1 in 70 AD. Later that year, the Romans attacked Jerusalem and completely destroyed the Temple. What makes all of this even more interesting is the fact that the solar eclipse on March 20 falls right in the middle of the blood moon tetrad, and it also happens to end the Shemitah year. Two Solar eclipses in a row of Nisan 1, is definitely marking an important year, I feel is the final year of God's creation, or year 6000. Eclipses on important biblical dates have been associated with key world events throughout history, as blood red moons are an omen of war for Israel.

Fig Tree: In Luke 21, Jesus speaks of watching these troubles, for a sign the New Age coming, like the Fig Tree casting first figs, to see when summer is near. Fruiting fig trees have a long juvenile period compared to other fruit trees. Most figs will not produce a crop for the first four to five years.

Fig trees produce two crops every year, but only one of them may be edible. The first crop, **(First Fruits)** called the breba crop, occurs relatively early in the year, in early summer, even as early as mid-winter. These fruits are frequently small, but may be useful for preservation.

The second crop occurs later in the year on the current year's growth and these figs should be ripe. These riper are ready to harvest during September, October, or November. The exact timing of the main crop depends on your climate and conditions.

My best and most educated guess is first the Rapture, on a Passover, (around March or April), and then the Second Coming three and a half years later on or around Trumpets, or Shacoat (September or October). And I feel He is telling me, both are on Shabbat days. So we had better study, when is His real appointed days? It is not Sundays, or even all Saturdays. It is from New Moon to New Moon. See Chapter 18 on "God's Appointed Worship Day."

Candlesticks: Revelation 1:12–13 shows Jesus is in the Midst of the Candlesticks, or the middle.

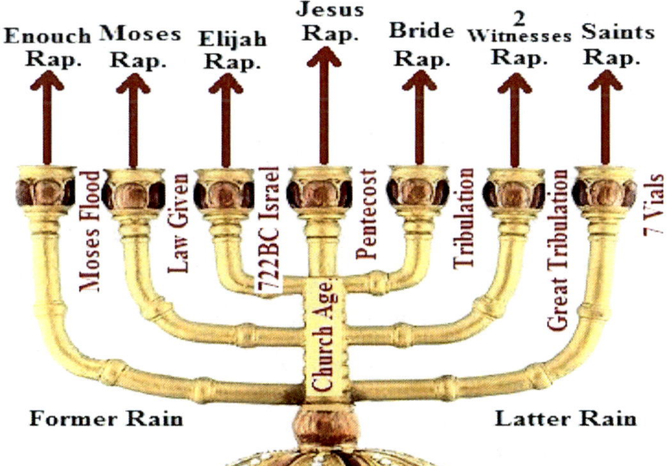

Rapture before major events.

The Temple of God is measured in Revelation 11:1–2, but the court was given to the Gentiles, or heathen. I see this as the Holy of Holies is for the Elect Bride. The Inner court is for the Saints, and the outer court is left to the dogs, for destruction.

Like the Showbread, rises in three measures. Matthew 13:33 The Kingdome of God is as a woman who hid a loaf in three measures, till the whole was leavened. Let it rise, beat it up, let it rise, beat it up, let it rise, and burn it.

My theory of Psalm 119 is that every year from 2000 on seems to mirror Psalm 100 on. So the year 2001 is Psalm 101, and the year 2007 is Psalm 107, and the year 2014 is Psalm 114, and on. I have noticed how very accurate the sayings of these chapters are to the adjoining years. So let's go look up what happens in Psalm 119, it blows up into the entire alphabet of the Jewish Hebrew language. The meaning of these letters put together, seem to speak of terror, and mayhem. You may have to do your own research.

It is then telling of the year 2019. So consider that thought, of what will happen then, in 2019? This theory also is consistent with the timeline suggested in this book, and the book "Zenith 2016," where he says the tribulation started in December 2012, and will finish seven years later, at the second coming. So 2016 would be mid tribulation, and the start of the Great tribulation.

Psalm 119 is the longest chapter of the Bible. It is divided into twenty-two sections, each titled after a letter of the twenty-two letters of the Hebrew alphabet. Each of these sections has eight verses.

1. ALEPH (Psalm 119:1–8)
2. BETH (Psalm 119:9–16)

3. GIMEL (Psalm 119:17–24)
4. DALETH (Psalm 119:25–32)
5. HE (Psalm 119:33–40)
6. VAU (Psalm 119:41–48)
7. ZAIN (Psalm 119:49–56)
8. CHETH (Psalm 119:57–64)
9. TETH (Psalm 119:65–72)
10. JOD (Psalm 119:73–80)
11. CAPH (Psalm 119:81–88)
12. LAMED (Psalm 119:89–96)
13. MEM (Psalm 119:97–104)
14. NUN (Psalm 119:105–112)
15. SAMECH (Psalm 119:113–120)
16. AIN (Psalm 119:121–128)
17. PE (Psalm 119:129–136)
18. TZADDI (Psalm 119:137–144)
19. KOPH (Psalm 119:145–152)
20. RESH (Psalm 119:153–160)
21. SCHIN (Psalm 119:161–168)
22. TAU (Psalm 119:169–176)

In studying the Greek alphabet, similarities pop out at me, because God uses it in Revelation when He makes known that He is the Alpha and the Omega, the beginning and the ending, the first and the last. I feel this is an important chapter.

Symbolic Meaning of the Hebrew Letters

In the First Gospel of the Infancy of Jesus Christ, a book well known to the Gnostics in the second century, is a story which has suggestions, as follows. This story is also held among the Persians, and is as follows:

There was also at Jerusalem one Zaccheus who was a schoolmaster; and he said to Joseph, Joseph, why does thou not send Jesus to me that he may learn his letters?

Joseph agreed and told St. Mary. So they brought him to that master; who, as soon as he saw him, wrote out an alphabet for him, and he bade him say Aleph; and when he had said Aleph, the master bade him say Beth. Then the Lord Jesus said to him, tell me first the meaning of the letter Aleph, and then I will pronounce the Beth.

And when the master threatened to whip him, the Lord Jesus explained to him the meaning of the letters Aleph and Beth; also which were the straight figures of the letters, which the oblique, and what letters had double figures; which had points, and which had none; why one letter went before another, and many other things he began to tell him, and explain, of which the master himself had never heard, nor read in any book.

The Lord Jesus further said to the master, take notice how I say to thee; then he began clearly and distinctly to say Aleph, Beth, Gimel, Daleth, and so on to the end of the alphabet. At this the master was so surprised, that he said, I believe this boy was born before Noah; and turning to Joseph, he said, Thou hast brought a boy to me to be taught, who is more learned than any master. The meanings are as Noah's day.

Greek interpretation: Hence ALPHA and OMEGA

LETTERS	INTERPRETATION
Alpha	Heavily break the waters
Beta	extending over the plains.
Gamma	They cover the land
Delta	in low places where
Epsilon	there are obstructions, shores form and whirlpools
Zeta	strike the earth
Eta	with water.
Theta	The water spreads
Iota	on all that lives and moves.
Kappa	Sediments give way.
Lambda	Submerged is the land
Mu	of Mu.
Ni	The peaks only
Xi	appear above the water.
Omikron	Whirlwinds blow around
Pi	by little and little
Rho	until comes
Sigma	cold air. Before
Tau	where existed valleys,
Upsilon	now, abysses, frozen tanks. In circular places
Phi	clay formed.
Chi	A mouth
Psi	opens, vapors
Omega	come forth — and volcanic sediments.

You can start to see Noah's story here.

The Greek alphabet is an intentional digression for the clearer understanding of the Hebrew alphabet, which must be reduced from symbols to words. Following table results:

NAME OF LETTERS	INTERPRETATION OF SYMBOL, WORD, OR LETTER Rendered in English
ALEPH	An Ox or Bullock, a sacrifice or at-one-ment. Its numerical value is ONE.
BETH	A House or Tent, a dwelling or tabernacle, in, among, within, etc.
GIMEL	A Camel, like a camel's hump, heap, collect, high.
DALETH	A Door or Gate, lid, valve.
HE	Lo, see, behold, (therefore) a lattice or window for that purpose
VAV	A Peg, Nail or Hook, therefore, wherefore, then, that, in order that, so that, etc.
ZAYIN	A Weapon, a shining sword, brightness, light.
CHETH	An Enclosure, fenced in, ark, refuge.
TETH	A Serpent, like a serpent, rolled, twisted, entwined.
YOD	The Hand, the **right hand, to strike or pierce**, a stroke, a blow.
KAPH	**The Hollow or Palm of the Hand**, curved, concave, a valley or basin.
LAMEDH	A Goad, towards, into, unto, until, upon, even to, besides, etc.
MEM	Water, waves, **a flood**.
NUN	A Fish, to sprout, to put forth, Noah, (as one from whom all are propagated).
SAMEKH	A Fulcrum, prop, lever, to help, to sustain, to uphold, the hinge of a **mason's apron,** a ladder or line connecting the lower with the higher, the Holy Ghost.
AYIN	The Eye, to flow, to flow out, a fountain.
PE	The Mouth, to breathe, to blow, a side or quarter of the heavens, region, part, quarter.

TSADHE	A Scythe or **Reaping-hook**, just, pertains to the harvest or retribution. Tsadok is Jupiter or justice (in Sanscrit, karma).
QOPH	Occiput**, back of the head, to move in a circle.**
RESH	Head, first, foremost, beginning, front. Rosh means a foremost or most northern nation.
SHIN	Tooth, **a sharp rock**, cliff, crag. The Almighty (Shaddi) if seen from the front, **but Satan if seen from behind.**
TAU	A Sign or **Mark,** cross, a symbol, a token.

This speaks of the Mark of the Beast in the meat of the right hand, Beast's head wound as in a circle on the back side of his head, a reaping hook, Masons, and flood. Makes you wonder, just saying.

Another theory is when considering the timing of Jesus coming, Daniel 12:11–12 tells us about the Abomination being set up in 1,290 days, and then the desolation, saying; "but blessed are those who wait till the 1,335th day." There are 45 days difference here, and this could be our only warning time.

Matthew 12:39 says, "No sign given but the sign of the prophet Jonas." This could be three days of darkness, from solar flares. Then these six weeks of no electricity at all, no cars, no phones, no stores open, no food or water etc. Maybe we should prepare for six weeks anyway.

This could be a time to be shut in for 6 weeks to reflect and pray, just before Jesus comes. Just saying. Or forty-five days of persecutions, of the Mark of the Beast.

I am quite sure the third Fatima prediction of Sister Lucia to the Vatican was of a polar shift, and this pending great destruction. Right after she told them, the Vatican opened up their own observatory. Now they say aliens could exist. Lucia told them to announce it to the world in 1960 but they did not. In 1960, Planet X, for the first time, could be seen by high resolution infrared rays. Scientists knew it was true. But they kept it a secret.

Many scientists have been killed by the CIA for trying to tell us about it. They know this planet is causing all our Earths birth panes, but they are blaming it on global warming. This is why they put out the Kemp Trails, in the sky, to track any abnormal changes quicker, so they can hide in their bunkers in time. They don't care about us.

Planet X and the Mysterious Death of Dr. Robert Harrington

YOWUSA.COM, 22-May-2008
John DiNardo
Janice Manning

Dr. Robert S. Harrington, the Chief astronomer of the U.S. Naval Observatory, died before he could publicize the fact that Planet X is approaching our Solar System.

Many feel his death part if a cover-up? One in which government agencies quickly moved to conceal the most earth-shaking discovery in history. If so, the search for truth begins in New Zealand.

CLUE: The Mayan December 2012 campaign was so big in the media it had to be a diversion. They knew nothing would happen yet, and hopped to get us to get discouraged and quit looking. If there were any truth they would have gone to great lengths to hide this information. But we never hear what they have to say about Planet X. They answer those questions in private, with a "not true!"

Another subject are crop circles. I feel this is a type of warning to us, but we are just not getting it. On the show *Ancient Aliens*, there was presented a magnetic rock with a similar pattern as one of these circles. This rock was found in the City of Roswell. It shows where two poles grab on both sides, and it is magnetic. It shows a large circle as an orbit, with Earth in the center, and near the orbit an eclipse is taking place, bigger Sun and Planet X. Then it shows the same *flipped* over on the other side. Just saying. What do you think?

Geometry of the 1996 crop formation:

18. GOD'S APPOINTED WORSHIP DAY

The Fourth Commandment.

The change in our Calendar is the devil's evil plot to stop our worship of God.

When the Holy Spirit woke me up to what evil was going on in this world, and then to the fact that Jesus was coming for his Bride very soon, I began to cry out to God, asking what more I had to do to be ready. Was there anything wrong I needed to change? The Holy Spirit told me to pray that I would be allowed to walk in the paths of old, the Ancient Paths. That seemed very strange to me, but I prayed to be allowed to walk in the Ancient Paths.

Early the very next morning I awoke with a download from God, saying that our present Calendars were perverted. The Lord explained that we were not supposed to worship Him on Sunday. I sat up in bed stunned, and I took the whole day doing research on Jewish worship. First I looked up the Jewish calendar, but all they did was worship on all Saturdays. I knew that was not right. So I researched what they did originally. I found that in Jesus day they worshiped on the Sabbath, using the New Moon as a monthly marker, and counted the days from then every month. That meant the original year is really eleven days short from ours today, every year. We do not even know the correct year either.

Luni-Solar Calendar						1
Day 1	Day 2	Day 3	Day 4	Day 5	Day 6	Sabbath
2	3	4	5	6	7	8
9	10	11	12	13	14	15
16	17	18	19	20	21	22
23	24	25	26	27	28	29
30						

The Lunar Cycle

The Jewish calendar is based on lunar cycles, from evening on one day, to the evening of the next day. Day 1: Toward the beginning of the moon's cycle, it appears as a thin crescent. That is the signal for a new Jewish month. Then we count seven days to Sabbath. The moon grows until it is full, the middle of the month, and then it begins to wane until it cannot be seen. It remains invisible for approximately two days, and then the thin crescent reappears, and the cycle begins again. All Sabbaths are always on the 8, 15, 22, and 29 days.

The entire cycle takes approximately 29½ days. Since a month needs to consist of complete days, a month is sometimes twenty-nine days long, and some are thirty.

Knowing exactly when the month begins has always been important in Jewish practice, because the Torah schedules the Jewish festivals according to the days of the month. The First day, Day 1, is always New Moon Day, and is set apart to celebrate the new month. Some work is allowed on this day.

The first day of the month as well as the thirtieth day of a *malei* month (almost every other month) is called *Rosh Chodesh*, the "Head of the Month," and has semi-festive rituals. But this is not Shabbat yet.

After every New Moon is set on the monthly calendar by the Priest, or Rabbi, then is counted seven days, four times, to get the Shabbat's, or Sabbath's day. See the example above. Then each month is started this way again.

So you can clearly see our calendar today, does not have a beginning or end. They just are run on linear. Also we have forced them to fit the yearly solar rotation of the Sun, adding days to our years.

We have longer years, and months. We go by the Sun, on days and years, and not the Moon. Day and night, not night and day. We worship on Sunday, the first of the week, and not the last. This is totally the opposite of what God wanted and is perverted.

THIS IS BIG. W-H-A-T?

Satan has stolen God's holy appointed worship day, absolutely all over the Earth, even with the Jews. Right under our noses. We are worshiping on the Sun god's day, a pagan deity.

You know, to worship on Gods Holy appointed Day, is one of the Ten Commandments, not a suggestion. And none of us do it, no not one.

So, come back to your first love. Really! No wonder we cannot hear God as well as they did in the Old Testament, or even in Jesus's day, when John wrote the book of Revelation. I have a small calendar to help convert at the end of the chapter. But you must do your own homework.

The Jewish Months

Nissan is the first month on the Jewish calendar. Before the Jews left Egypt, on the first day of the month of Nissan, God told Moses and Aaron: "This *chodesh* [new moon, or month] shall be to you the head of months."Thus the peculiarity of the Jewish calendar: the year begins on *Rosh Hashanah*, the first day of the month of *Tishrei* (the anniversary of the creation of Adam and Eve), but Tishrei is not the first month. Rosh Hashanah is actually referred to in the Torah as "the first day of the seventh month."

CLUE: So here again God points out these two times of year, around Passover and Sukkot. Huuum! Right?

The Jewish Months and their Special Dates

Jewish Month	Approximate Secular Date	This Month's Special Dates
Nissan	March–April	Passover
Iyar	April–May	Lag B'Omer
Sivan	May–June	Shavuot
Tammuz	June–July	
Menachem Av	July–August	Tisha B'Av
Elul	August–September	

Tishrei	September–October	The High Holidays (Rosh Hashanah andYom Kippur), Sukkot, Shmini Atzeret, andSimchat Torah
Marcheshvan	October–November	
Kislev	November–December	Chanukah
Tevet	December–January	Conclusion of Chanukah
Shevat	January–February	Tu B'Shvat
Adar	February–March	Purim

Throughout the generation, we have lost the exact months to get the correct holidays. But to our best calculations, scholars have determined that September 2014 to September 2015 must be the Jewish year 6000.

All we can do now is *repent* to God for what we have done and start acknowledging the Sabbaths again, till Jesus comes. Expect to hear from God. We can still meet with others at church because of the scripture below.

> Not forsaking the assembling of ourselves together, as the manner of some is; but exhorting one another: and so much the more, as ye see the day approaching. **(Heb 10:25)**

But, don't forget His appointed worship days. No man can judge how you worship on these days, but you can see that Jesus and the disciples did worship on these days.

> Let no man therefore judge you in meat, or in drink, or in respect of a holyday, or of the new moon, or of the sabbath days: **(Col 2:16)**

Observing the moon today: Notably, there are some changes happening from the normal years ago. The lunar shadings in the past were always right and left crescents a seen in the lunar chart below. Half-moons were on the sides. But today in 2014 we see it on the bottom, shown here, which is proving our poles are shifting.

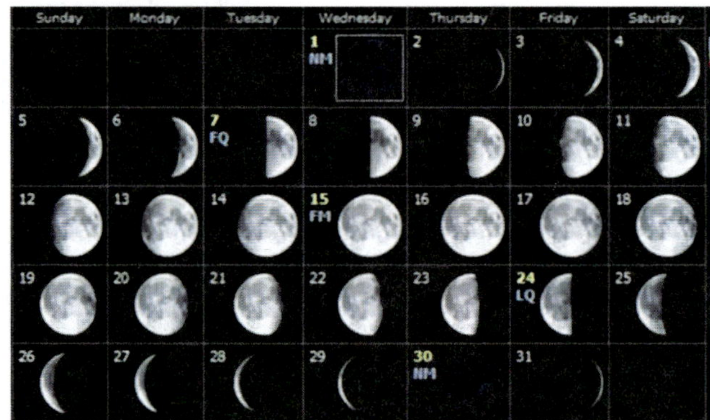

Then,

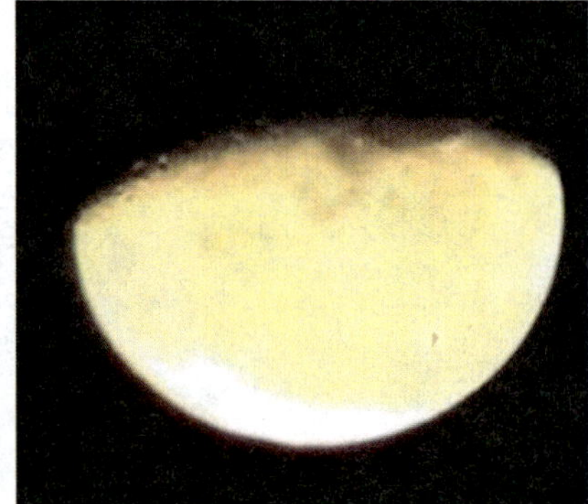

and what now 2014?

2015 ☐ Blue is SABBATH DAY = The Evening before and that day.

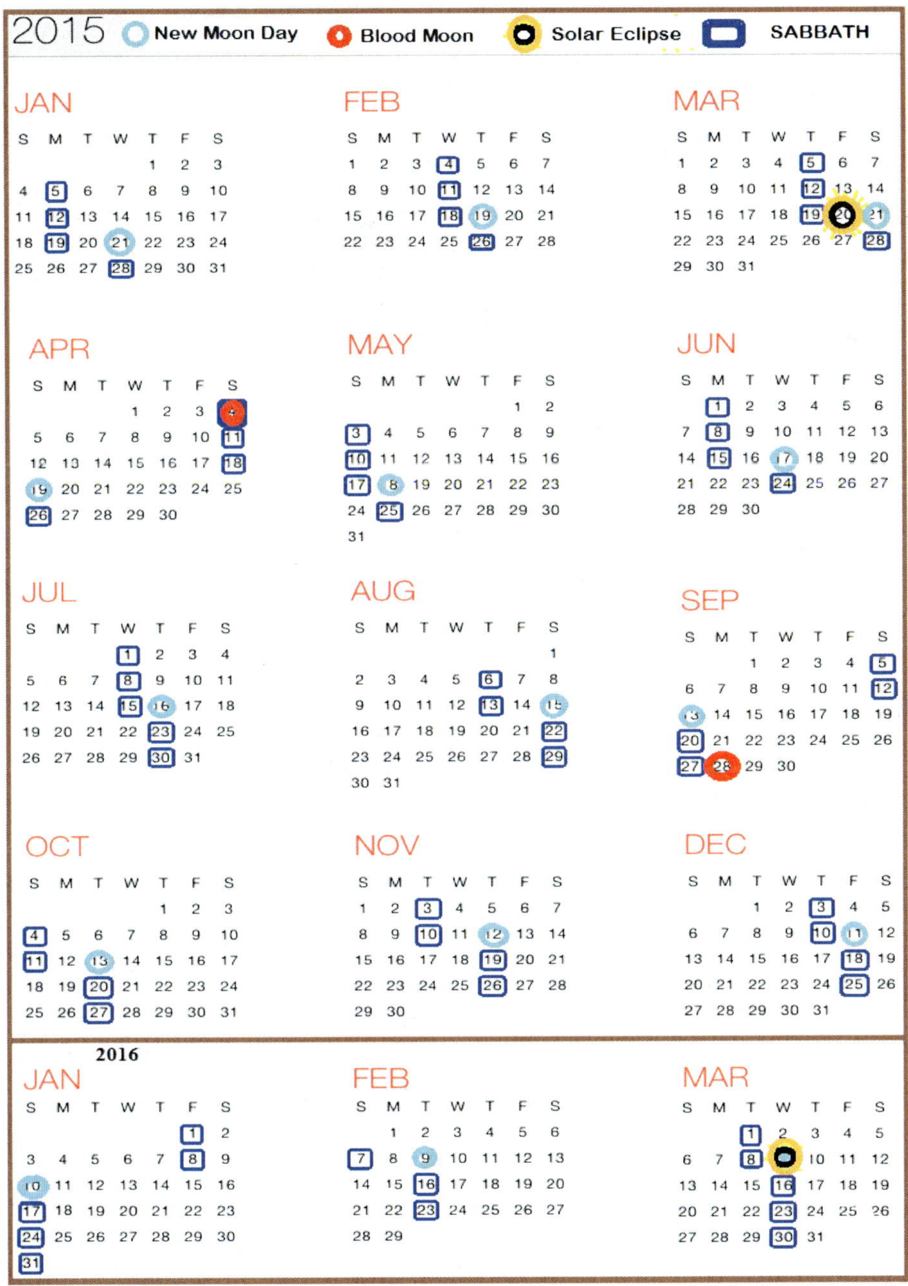

19. AFTERWORD

Prepare the way for the coming of the lord Jesus Christ in absolute repentance, righteousness, holiness, truth and complete surrender to the lord Jesus Christ (Yehoshua ha mashiach). Time is absolutely over; the messiah Jesus Christ is imminently coming to pick up his bride! (See John 3:16).

An example of a REPENTANCE PRAYER:

Jesus, please forgive me of all my sins. I believe in you, and what you did for me on the cross. I declare today that you are my Lord and Savior, and I repent and turn away from all sin.

Please cover me with your precious blood, and establish your word in my life, that I may be found in righteousness and holiness, and write my name in your book of life. Baptize me with the power of the Holy Spirit, that I can be taught the truth. In the mighty name of Jesus Christ. Holy Spirit you are welcome, come teach me the truth.

Amen.

Here are some scriptures; you may use to pray over your children, Spiritual Children, or family: Acts 16:31, 1 Corinthians 7:14, Isaiah 59:21, Psalms 91:9–10, Proverbs 31:28.

20. ABOUT THE AUTHOR

Rev. Rose Jacques

I have been ministering for about twenty-eight years. This is my story in short:

When I was five years old, I spoke French. My dad died in a work accident. While my mom and siblings were grieving, an angel was there holding my hand. That was the first time I saw an angel. Since then I have seen many angels.

My mother, still trying to cope, sent my seven-year-old sister and I to live at the convent with the nuns a couple of years. I felt as orphaned as anyone, but drew close to God, as He was the one I felt was there for me then. When I lost my earthly father, God faithfully became my Father. The nuns took us to church every day, without fail. This went on that whole time, and I drew even closer to God. Having had a close relationship with my father before he died, getting close to Father God was easy. I learned at an early age to hear God, but I always knew I was different. I never forgot God, and He never forgot me.

When I was twelve, I cried out to God, "Please, God, don't let my life be a waste." Soon after, I was going to school, when some girls were purposed to beat me up, one girl swinging at me. It was as if her arm went through my body, and never made contact. This scared them off. As I entered the school, I saw a giant man, ten or eleven feet tall, in the hall, reaching on top of the lockers to get some books, his head bent because of the ceiling. I noted all the young teens were there but they could not see him. These cruel kids did not react to this stranger. All the kids were up to his belt buckle in height. As he started to turn around to look at me, I ran off afraid to talk, thinking I was impolite by staring. When I grew up, I was to understand he was my Guardian Angel, who went to school with me, and there to protect me. When other kids played ball, I was alone at home playing, as if I was building an orphanage, and adopting thousands of kids. I grew up to become a heavy soul winner, and learned to adopt many into the Kingdom of God.

All through my young age, I have seen angels, and when I received the Holy Spirit at twenty-seven, there was a very large owl the size of my five-year-old son in my home tree for thirty days and nights. I did not understand what was happening to me for many years. So I just kept it to myself, but now I hope to impact some with my testimony, especially now time is short, and evil abounds. I feel the owl is a symbol of screeching to warn all the critters in the forest when evil is present, prophetically.

I assure you God, the angels, and Jesus are real. God answers prayer, but His way. If you have not experience God or Jesus, then you are probably not praying.

I have been a pastor and am now in short-term missions. I have gone to China, the Philippines, many African countries, Israel, Jordan, Haiti, etc. God has been good to me. Recently God has been talking to me about the Book of Revelation, and the end times. I have been given the gift of wisdom, to understanding the whole Book. I pray this book now can bless you. Jesus is really coming, so get excited.

Rose Jacques

"DILIGENT HARVESTERs"

A SOUL WINNING TEACHING

"AND THE SPIRIT AND THE BRIDE SAY COME"

12 Teachings geared to train any sized group to be effective in their community.

We show you how to start a Soul Winning Group. This series is sure to grow your group, with helpful tips on how to follow up. We provide an excellent teaching to equip and train the evangelists in your church or community, to win the lost, based on the great commission.

For the legal rights to distribute or translate this book in another language, please contact us with a request. Time is short, please join us in this effort to get the word out. God Bless

Order this book "*Unlocking Revelation*" or the Audio or CD "Diligent Harvesters" series at: unlockingrevelation.tateauthor.com

listen|imagine|view|experience

AUDIO BOOK DOWNLOAD INCLUDED WITH THIS BOOK!

In your hands you hold a complete digital entertainment package. In addition to the paper version, you receive a free download of the audio download of this book. Simply use the code listed below when visiting our website. Once downloaded to your computer, you can listen to the book through your computer's speakers, burn it to an audio CD or save the file to your portable music device (such as Apple's popular iPod) and listen on the go!

How to get your free audio download:

1. Visit www.tatepublishing.com and click on the e|LIVE logo on the home page.
2. Enter the following coupon code: d71d-5335-941a-592e-4146-ba0e-c14a-465b
3. Download the audio download from your e|LIVE digital locker and begin enjoying your new digital entertainment package today!

THE BRIDEGROOM IS COMING

A DIVINELY INSPIRED EXHAUSTIVE STUDY UNVEILING THE ENTIRE BOOK OF REVELATION

Rev. Rose was given a dream of the rapture after the first of the recent 4 blood moons, in 2014. Receiving many visions to follow, she was inspired to share what God was telling her about the Book of Revelation and the soon return of the Bridegroom, Jesus Christ. It is the full explanation of the Book of Revelation.

In this book, Rev. Rose shares what God has told her of Jesus coming, her visions, what is expected of his Bride, and God's true worship days. She adds some of her personal theories of prophetic timing she has come to know.

"AND THE SPIRIT AND THE BRIDE SAY COME"

Rev. Rose Jacques has evangelized worldwide for 28 years and has pastored and advised many pastors. After hearing from the Lord of Jesus's eminent coming, having dreams and visions, she was aspired to write this book of the full meaning of the Book of Revelation. She has seen many miracles and can attest that God is real. It is time to wake up and follow the Holy Spirit.